Leading with Nothing to Lose

Leading with Nothing to Lose

Training in the Exercise of Power

Book 2 of
THE UNDEFENDED LEADER trilogy

Simon Walker

PiQUANT
editions

British Library Cataloguing in Publication Data

Walker, Simon
 Leading with nothing to lose : training in the exercise of
 power. - (The undefended leader trilogy ; bk. 2)
 1. Leadership 2. Power (Social sciences)
 I. Title
 303.3'4

Other titles in Simon Walker's The Undefended Leader trilogy, are

Leading out of Who You Are:
Discovering the Secret of Undefended Leadership
(Piquant Editions, ISBN 978-1-903689-43-1)

Leading with Everything to Give:
Disarming the Powers and Authorities
(forthcoming August 2008; ISBN 978-1-903689-45-5)

Cover design by Philip Miles
Book design by To a Tee (www.2at.com)

To my parents

Contents

Preface ix
1 The Power of Weakness: the Overlooked Source 1

Part I: The Ecology of Power
2 A Choice of Forces: Front Stage or Back Stage? 9
3 A Choice of Forces: Strong or Weak? 16
4 A Choice of Forces: Expanding or Consolidating? 21
5 Combining Forces 26

Part II: The Eight Strategies of Power in an Organization
6 Abraham Lincoln and the Foundational Strategy (RSC) 35
7 Franklin D Roosevelt and the Commanding Strategy (PSC) .45
8 Ronald Reagan and the Affiliative Strategy (PWX) 58
9 Jimmy Carter and the Serving Strategy (RWX) 68
10 Winston Churchill and the Pacesetting Strategy (PSX) 79
11 Martin Luther King and the Visionary Strategy (RSX) 89
12 Nelson Mandela and the Consensual Strategy (PWC) 100
13 Jesus and the Self-Emptying Strategy (RWC) 113

Part III: Undefended Power
14 Finding the Holy Grail of Leadership 125
15 Leading with Nothing to Lose: the Key to Mobility 137
16 The Hospitality of the Undefended Leader 144

Appendix: Troubleshooting Problems in Leadership and
          Other FAQs 151
Select Bibliography 157
The Leadership Community and
          Leadership Signature Profile™ 159

List of Diagrams

2.1   Front- and backstage forces 12
3.1   Strong and weak forces in a situation 18
4.1   Expanding and consolidating forces 24
5.1   The Leadership Strategy model 30
6.1   Foundational (RSC) action and PWX reaction 40
7.1   Commanding (PSC) action and RWX reaction. 55
8.1   Affiliative (PWX) action and RSC reaction 65
9.1   Serving (RWX) action and PSC reaction 76
10.1 Pacesetting (PSX) action and RWC reaction 86
11.1 Visionary (RSX) action and PWC reaction 97
12.1 Consensual (PWC) action and RSX reaction 110
13.1 Self-emptying (RWC) action and PSX reaction. 121
14.1 The characteristics of McIndoe's leadership 130
16.1 The dynamics of hosting 146

Preface

Leading with Nothing to Lose, the second book in the trilogy The Undefended Leader, continues where *Leading out of Who You Are* left off. If you have not read that first book, perhaps it will help if I give you a very brief résumé of its central ideas. Here it is, in two paragraphs.

Leadership involves power and influence over others, and it is incumbent upon a leader to use that power and influence benignly. However, each of us is trapped by a psychological imperative which was shaped during our childhood and which is at the root of our very ego, our sense of self. It is the source of our drives and fears. I identified four particular ego patterns (called Shaping, Defining, Adapting and Defending) and showed how they determine the personal needs we will be prone to try to meet in our lives as leaders. The greater the pressure to meet those needs, the more 'defended' we become.

One of the principal strategies we develop to defend our selves is to divide our leadership performance between a 'front stage' and a 'back stage'. This allows us to either reveal or conceal certain aspects of our selves, to manage audiences we see as potentially threatening. We can become less defended only if our perception of that audience changes: from being intimidating, critical or dismissive to being unconditionally and reliably affirming. This cannot be simply a matter of believing something we know is untrue; we need genuinely to find a new audience that has that characteristic. The best human audiences (secure relationships, loving marriages, deep friendships and so forth) can go some way towards fulfilling that need, but ultimately we have to find a spiritual source of approval if we are to be set free. The undefended life is available only to those who can locate such a source and learn to pay attention to it. This is the calling of the undefended leader.

However, the journey to undefended leadership does not stop there. Locating the source of freedom is only the beginning of the path, not the end, which has to lead, in practice, to a new approach to the tasks of leadership. And so we come to the second part of the trilogy, which you are holding in your hands. *Leading with Nothing to Lose* travels on into the territory of the leader who has to make hard-nosed executive decisions every day: managing budgets, setting targets, hiring and firing personnel, negotiating conflict, improving performance, organising procedures, planning strategy, getting his hands dirty in the bump and grind of routine leadership.

If *Leading out of Who You Are* dealt with the fundamentals of the person of the leader, *Leading with Nothing to Lose* deals with the fundamentals of their power. The practicalities of leadership are just as important as the ethics and ideals. These things are, rightly and necessarily, bedfellows and the aim of this book is to get them back under the quilt together: an undefended leader with undefended tools of leadership who is inspired by an undefended vision.

Simon Walker
Oxford, 2007

ONE

The Power of Weakness: the Overlooked Source

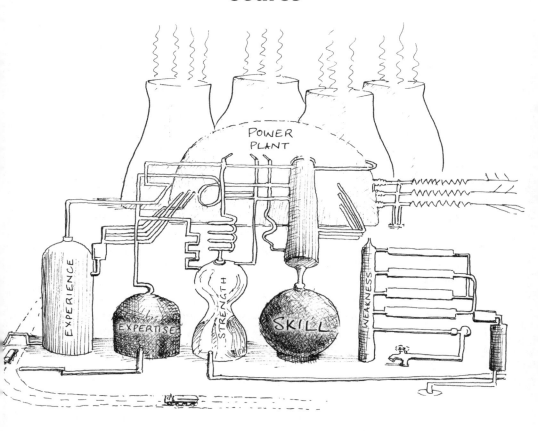

Most of us have, at some stage in our lives, discovered that being weak does not always mean being powerless. We probably stumbled on this realization unexpectedly, for our instinct and culture alike tend to tell us that the reverse is true—that to be weak means to be ineffectual and at the mercy of others. Imagine, for example, someone advertising a seminar on 'How being weak can make you strong'. You won't find this class being taught in Basic Military

Theory, or on an MBA course in business management. You will find plenty of sessions on how to be more effective, how to be more productive, how to be more potent in your leadership. You'll find dozens of courses offering you ways to build up your portfolio of skills or develop a more influential social network. You'll find courses on time management and 'personal impact skills'; but you'll struggle to find a single class that suggests that learning to be weak may actually be a part of being strong—and not just *quite* strong but the strongest a person can be.

And yet, nonetheless, I would bet you have had experiences in your life that might suggest that sometimes, in certain situations, the weakest person can actually be the most powerful. Maybe it was as a small child, when you discovered that even though you were the smallest member of your family, the one with the least education and the emptiest piggy bank, you could get your own way—just by screaming. Or maybe it was when you were sick and were let off school, and your whole day was transformed as the dread of the spelling test lifted and for 12 hours the world revolved around you. Your mum took the day off work and you were waited on, soothed and allowed to lounge in bed—simply because you croaked and whispered and shivered.

Maybe, if you are a woman, it was when you discovered that men will stop and spend hours helping you if you stand by your car staring anxiously into the engine and looking flustered and helpless. Or maybe it was when you realized that sometimes it is better to lose a battle than to win it but lose the war. Or that sometimes it's better to waive your rights and so demonstrate your moral superiority, or to give away something precious and so win a friend for life.

Perhaps in a history class you learned about the Norman conquest of England in 1066. Remember how the Saxon king Harold met the invading army of William at Hastings in the famous battle that was to be recorded on the Bayeux Tapestry? Harold's troops occupied the higher ground and had the upper hand when they saw the Normans falling back in apparent defeat. The Saxons charged down the hill after them, only to find themselves enveloped in an ambush. The Norman retreat had been a ruse, a pretence of weakness intended to lure the Saxons into a trap. And it worked.

Perhaps in the gym, practising judo, you mastered the 'sacrifice throw' of *tio toshi*, rolling back onto the ground and using your opponent's forward momentum to propel him over your head. The sight of his adversary falling to the ground, apparently overwhelmed, tempts him into a final surge, an overbalance—and the very opposite of the outcome he was expecting. In fact, judo throws almost all exploit the 'advantage' of your opponent, their weight and power, and use it against them.

Perhaps you watched the celebrated 'Rumble in the Jungle' between Muhammad Ali and George Foreman on 30 October 1974. Ali, the underdog who had lost his heavyweight title, faced the much younger, larger and stronger Foreman, a brutal puncher who literally bludgeoned his opponents into submission. Ali carried off a magnificent victory against all the odds by allowing Foreman to batter him for most of the fight as he leant back on the ropes, absorbing unimaginable punishment. When Foreman's strength was eventually spent, Ali launched his own brilliant counter-attack in the eighth round and knocked his demoralized opponent out on his feet.

Or perhaps you observed the final years and months of the life of the previous pope, John Paul II. As the world looked on, this frail, bent and feeble old man made his way towards his own death. And yet, in those closing weeks, larger crowds than ever gathered outside the Vatican to catch a glimpse of him on the balcony, and people spoke of the inspiration he gave them, the power they sensed in him, though he had never been weaker or less able to speak. It seemed that, when almost all human strength had left him, he had found strength from another source that transcended human limitations.

These are not isolated examples. In fact, when you think about it, weakness is often more powerful than strength. Of course, you could object that sometimes the power of weakness seems to lie in manipulation and cunning, subversive actions that are not altogether honourable or even honest in intent—and that may indeed be the case. Weakness, just as much as strength, can be used for ignoble purposes. But there is nothing inherently bad about the force of weakness. Like strength, it is a question of what it is used to achieve.

Weakness can be so potent it can pierce the most hardened of hearts, so forceful it can break through any resolve, so appealing it can win more allies, funds and support than all the marketing campaigns in the world. More than that, it can achieve different kinds of things that strength can never achieve, as we will discover in this book. It isn't just that it can be strong, it's that it can exert a particular kind of strength, a particular type of power, that simply is not available from any other source. There are things that can only be accomplished through the exercise of weakness.

It is somewhat strange, therefore, that weakness is so little talked of in books about leadership. Those that have sold in their millions, that line the shelves of every executive's office in the developed world, do so because they talk about strength, and about power. They explain how to become more effective, how to run the show faster and sleeker and for greater profit. They give away secrets of how to win and they promise success to those who obey their rules.

However, they allow very little space for any consideration of the power of weakness. Why is this? Surely, if weakness is a kind of power—and we all know it is, because all of us have used it at some time in our lives to great effect—then it ought to feature in discussions about leadership. The answer, of course, is that weakness is threatening. I remember a course I led for some senior leaders.

One of them, who ran a large, thriving organization, looked at me in disbelief when I suggested that they should allow weakness to be expressed on his staff team. 'That would be a disaster!' he objected. 'We wouldn't get any work done. Every board meeting would be reduced to a therapy session. I'd have people in floods of tears all the time. How would that be productive?'

That reaction is typical of many leaders. If I talk about the value of weakness, they feel: 'What does that say about all the macho stuff I pump up my troops with at the beginning of each quarter? If I start talking about weakness, I'm going to have an office full of weeping and wailing, of workers sharing all their failings and limitations. If I start talking about weakness, *I* may have to start showing some—and then I'll have a mutiny: I'll have people taking advantage, using my weakness against me. Before I know it, I'll lose control— I'll be upstaged, I'll be out. No, weakness is far too messy, too dangerous, too complicated and threatening to let out of the box. Better to keep it nailed up and pretend it doesn't exist. Sure, we can't get rid of it completely, but we can make damn sure we keep the lid on it as tightly as possible!'

Many leaders—though not all—are terrified of weakness. They see it only as something negative, both in themselves and in their followers. And what frightens them most deeply is what they might lose. They see their leadership as a medieval lord might have regarded his castle: as their own realm, in which they can do as they choose. Through strength, skill, hard work (and maybe birthright), a feudal lord won power and would build a stronghold to subdue those who would take it from him. His castle protected everything that was valuable to him: his wife, his children, his money, his lands, his serfs, his reputation. In a similar way, most leaders today regard themselves as defending their territory and the privileges that come with it. Their banner flies from their high towers and they will see off all intruders and assailants. Indeed, they suspect that most people around them, though they may call themselves allies, colleagues and friends, are secretly rivals or rebels in waiting. Everyone who has not actually worked their way inside their castle walls to feed from their table is out there plotting how to overthrow them. That's why many leaders surround themselves with people less talented than themselves and many choose sycophants as followers. It's why many maintain such control over their organizations, in case a threat should emerge beneath them that they were not aware of. Most leaders—though not all—are heavily defended and insist to themselves that only the best defended can survive.

We tried out the title for this trilogy on a number of leaders in business and politics. We'd ask: 'Imagine you saw a book on the shelf in Borders or Barnes & Noble entitled *The Undefended Leader*. Would you take it down?' Almost without exception they said they would, out of curiosity. Then, we asked them what they thought the book would be about. 'Well,' one would reply, 'I would think it was about a leader who had landed themself in a bit of trouble—you know, lacked back-up and support.' Or another would say, 'My guess is it would be a leader who didn't clearly know where he was going.' Or another: 'I'm not sure quite what the book would be saying, but I do know I wouldn't want to be that leader. He's vulnerable!'

For many men and some women, the idea of weakness is unthinkable: it's the very contradiction of all they believe in. They assume that being undefended is a negative thing, that it spells trouble. They assume that all leaders are trying to be as defended as possible. They expect books on leadership to explain how to become better defended, more competent, fitter, faster, stronger. Yet, at its most basic, leadership is concerned simply with the application of power to exert influence, to achieve things. Leaders need every tool they can lay their hands on to do the best job possible—and if weakness is one of the tools in the kit, they need to know about it. And not only know about it, but understand what it does and how and when to use it.

One of the tasks of this book is to take the risk of hauling up that box from wherever you have buried it, prising open the lid and taking a good look inside. And what we will find in there is a whole new way of thinking about power. What we are going to discover is that not only is weakness a source of power but there are seven other distinct kinds of power, which work in different ways and are appropriate and available for different situations.

Imagine if I told you there was a new source of energy that had the potential to revolutionize our lives and solve the global energy crisis. You might say, 'Great! Where can I get some?' Imagine if you were not just a consumer of energy but a supplier. In fact, imagine if you were the CEO of one of the biggest energy suppliers in the country. How would you react when I told you of this new source of energy? You'd say, 'Well, Mr Walker, that's very interesting, but I'd like to know a little more. Where's the evidence that this new energy source is more efficient? Has it ever been used before? How do we know it's safe? How expensive is it to harness? How much of it is there and why haven't the geologists or physicists told us about it before? I want to know a bit more about this new source of energy before I take this any further.'

And that would be fair enough. These are appropriate questions for someone to ask who is charged with the responsibility of supplying energy to millions of people. Their choices will affect thousands of businesses and hundreds of thousands of homes. They need to be properly informed. Just the practicalities will usually be enough for the consumer, who is probably most concerned about whether the new source of energy will cut their bills a little; but for the expert who has to manage this power professionally, only a rigorous understanding will do.

Now, the same is true of those of us who are called to be leaders in wider social situations. Like that CEO in the energy industry, we have at our disposal large sources of power to influence the lives of other people—in some cases, of many other people, even millions. It might be acceptable if we were merely consumers of power to say, 'Weakness? Great! That's a new one I must try some time.' But for those of us in leadership the only responsible choice is first to try to understand it a little better. What exactly is weakness? And, for that matter, what is strength? What do they do to people around them? Do they always work the same way? How do they relate to other forms of power? Can they be controlled? Are they dangerous? What are the safeguards we need to have in place? How do we access them appropriately?

If we want to be effective leaders, we will find it worthwhile to get an understanding not only of weakness but also of power: its source, its structure and its very nature. The aim of this book is to try to do just that. There are hundreds of books on leadership available, and many of them refer to the use of power; but there are rather fewer that actually dissect what power is. This book attempts to analyse its structure. In the next few chapters we will look at the key elements of power, the particular forces involved in any transaction. Then, having established the basic elements, we will go on to look at how they combine to form *patterns* of power. Rather than seeing these in terms of architecture (which might be appropriate if we were talking about physical forces applied to physical structures), we will use the image of an ecology of power, because the forces in play are social and the structure being built is not physical but social and emotional.

Once we have understood how the ecology of power is put together from its basic elements, it then becomes possible for the leader to learn how to combine these forces strategically. Throughout this book, you will find stories, illustrations and applications to explain how and when to use a particular strategy and what it can achieve. There are eight different strategies, and they have been represented powerfully by eight significant historical leaders: Abraham Lincoln, Franklin D Roosevelt, Ronald Reagan, Jimmy Carter, Winston Churchill, Martin Luther King, Nelson Mandela and Jesus of Nazareth.

The book ends by considering how leaders can progress from using perhaps one or two of these strategies to the freedom and mobility to use them all. We will explore the idea that, while to some extent this freedom can be achieved by practice, more fundamentally it is connected with the freedom to 'lead with nothing to lose'. And I shall suggest that the one essential characteristic of all the most mobile, flexible and ultimately effective leaders is that they have been undefended.

PART I

THE ECOLOGY OF POWER

TWO

A Choice of Forces: Front Stage or Back Stage?

It was Alexander Pope who said, 'The proper study of Mankind is Man.' We might adapt that dictum and suggest that the 'proper study' of the leader is the follower. If as leaders we are to research anything, the most worthwhile thing to investigate is the nature of the people we seek to influence. Until we understand that, we will not understand what we are doing at all.

Another way to look at this is to consider that power is the application of force in a human system. A leader exercises power in order to achieve an effect. Just as on a bicycle the power of our legs is applied as a physical force through the pedals to the wheels, so a leader applies social and emotional force through various mechanisms to the system of the human community in which they operate. That force has an effect, just as the force applied by pedalling a bike does. Just as the bike is set in motion, so the human system is set in motion by the force applied by the leader. Like a professional cyclist, the leader must therefore train herself to be able to exert the maximum force, and to do it in the right way and at the right time. There is no point applying full power all the time—indeed, it could be fatal if you were going round a sharp bend. Power without control can be lethal. The cyclist has an instinctive appreciation of the physics of the system and therefore knows how to apply power to the mechanisms of their bike appropriately and successfully.

What is the human system within which the leader applies force? Unlike the bike, it is held together not by physical bolts and nuts but by emotional and contractual ties, whether they be formal or informal. Those ties may be familial: a family is a human system in which a group of individuals are interconnected and bound together, by their genetic and cultural heritage, the emotional and legal bonds between them and their recognition as a group by the wider community. An event that affects one member of the family ultimately affects them all. Those ties may be contractual: a company is a human system in which, through formal, legal bonds, individuals make a commitment to expend a proportion of their time, energy and skills in a shared enterprise for the good of the system. Those ties may be ideological: a faith group is a human system in which, through informal but shared spiritual and historical perspectives, a group of individuals see themselves as bound together, with a common cause. Such bonds, though not legal, can often be as strong as (if not stronger than) those enshrined in law and contract, because they draw on deeper resources such as willpower, hope, trust and love. Finally, those ties may be aspirational: a sports team is a human system in which, through a common aspiration not just to play the same sport but to win the competition, a group of individuals participate in shared activities and disciplines.

Each of these human systems is different, but the kinds of forces that can be applied to each are the same. The leader must choose which force they will apply, and when. They have to decide

- whether to use front- or back-stage force
- whether to use strong or weak force
- whether to use expanding or consolidating force.

I will explain these terms as we look at each of these choices in turn in this and the next two chapters.

Front stage or back stage?

In 1960, Dwight Eisenhower's term as the 34th president of America came to an end, and the candidates who emerged to succeed him were his vice-president, Richard Nixon, and John F Kennedy. It was to be the first campaign in which television played a significant role,as in September and October of that year Nixon and Kennedy engaged in the first televized presidential debates. Nixon sweated under the lights and looked tense and ill-at-ease, but his opponent, groomed for power, influence and attention as a member of a political dynasty, was composed, confident and fluent. Unlike Nixon, the image-conscious and visually astute Kennedy came across as cool and collected. Those who heard the debates on the radio generally thought either that Nixon had won them or that the two men were equally matched; but those who watched them on television tended to find Kennedy the winner.

This outcome illustrates well the distinction between the use of force on the front stage and on the back. Kennedy was a classic exponent of the front stage. He was instinctively aware of his audience and their perception of him, and knew what was needed to manage their impression of him. Years of small talk at cocktail parties had prepared him for the easy, relaxing chat that appealed to the new visual medium, a medium that presents its viewers with the surface. The camera invites us to focus on what appears within its frame, encouraging us to think that what we can see is all there is to reality. Like visual theatre, TV offers us a captivating front stage, in which we are convinced by the characters, the action and the props we see before us. The medium is best suited to entertainment rather than education—documentaries tend to focus on visual information and padding and are sparsely annotated with dialogue, which must be pared down and simple. Television is a prime example of the front stage, and Kennedy was one of the first politicians to exploit it.

In contrast, Nixon remained wedded to older forms of communication and debate involving rhetoric, analysis and argument. Such methods, developed over many centuries, derive from cultures in which communication was largely verbal and the visual, if it was used at all, was mere illustration to add a little life. Like a traditional preacher, Nixon sought to compel his audience through force of argument. Unlike his opponent, he paid little attention to his appearance and refused to wear make-up. Instead, he concentrated on what one might call the 'backstage' elements of any communication: sound preparation, thorough reasoning. Like a well-organized producer, he had an effective backstage machine, well-planned, well-financed and well-rehearsed, which he believed would prove his substance to the audience and win their votes. The radio audience, who engaged mostly with the argument, were mostly convinced. However, for the TV audience, captivated by the front stage, it was like being taken on a tour of the backstage area of a theatre—important, no doubt, but not what most people would pay to see. They knew that this stuff was necessary, but they didn't want to have to understand it all. They took the gamble that behind the polished set of Kennedy's front stage, the back stage was in good order. Whether they were right or not is another question—and one whose answer history never allowed us to find out, of course.

The **front stage** (presented) is what is explicit, visible, on the surface—eg tangible relationships, status symbols, group tasks and goals.

The **back stage** (reserved) is what is implicit, hidden or buried from sight—eg assumptions, visions, convictions, boundaries, resources and secrets.

Diagram 2.1: Front- and backstage forces

Every leader must be aware that they can apply force on either the front or the back stage. These two approaches are very different, and so are their effects. The back stage involves activities such as negotiation, research, intelligence; the front stage, on the other hand, involves the public agreement after the negotiation, the product delivered at the end of the research, the campaign that is fought after the intelligence has come in. A good leader is in command of the overall theatre of his organization, community or society, and for this to function well he must be able to perform effectively on both the front stage and the back. Frontstage leadership addresses the visible and tangible aspects of a situation and its explicit concerns; backstage leadership addresses the foundations of a situation and its hidden assumptions and implicit concerns.

Very often, frontstage leadership is a social activity, involving the management of relationships. Very often, it involves conversation. Often, it is an 'output activity'—it focuses on the outputs of the task, not the inputs. Very often, it is concerned with the results of decisions, and determines the process that lies ahead. Here are some examples of this kind of leadership:

- A coach at the football club setting out the team's targets in the league that season
- A consultant surgeon in the operating theatre deciding who his team will be and organizing the operation
- A mother at the lunch table establishing a consensus amongst her children about whether to go to the park or the library that afternoon
- A salesman persuading a customer to buy the latest laptop
- A teacher encouraging and inspiring a group of students to come up with better ideas in a science project for Speech Day
- A executive making a decision to dismiss a member of staff for gross misconduct
- A conductor leading his orchestra through Beethoven's Fifth Symphony

On the other hand, backstage leadership is often less directive than frontstage leadership. Often, it's quiet, unnoticed and in the background. Often, it involves providing a kind of support, whether moral or emotional or practical. Often, it relates to preparation or inspiration for a future event. It provides the basis for a successful delivery on the front stage. It's usually concerned with inputs into a situation, such as teaching, agreeing, planning or saving, rather than outputs. Here are some examples of backstage leadership:

- A family reaching agreement on what behaviour is or is not acceptable in the home
- A husband doing the washing up after the dinner party while the others have coffee
- A wife sorting out the finances of a holiday in advance
- A coach teaching the basketball team the basics of dribbling so they can practise on their own
- A woman accompanying a friend to an important meeting to provide moral support

- A head teacher preparing an inspirational speech for the first staff meeting of term...

- ...or planning the curriculum for the new school year over the summer

Arguably, backstage leadership is more self-effacing than frontstage leadership. The frontstage leader accepts the challenge and responsibility of 'performing on stage'. She will be the one in the spotlight if things go wrong; she will be the visible face of success or failure. There is no hiding on the front stage. In contrast, backstage leadership takes responsibility but in a way that does not control the outputs on the front stage. A backstage leader such as a film producer may ensure that all the finance for the production has been secured and all the rehearsals organized, but it is the director who will ultimately oversee the performances of the actors on the front stage. The director gets the glory, while the producer may be the unsung hero.

In every situation there is always a back and a front stage, and leadership is necessary on both. Leaders who lead only on the front stage will be in danger of running out of resources, supplies and inputs backstage. After a while, their followers will feel tired, hungry or stressed because nothing is being put into the back stage—of the project, the followers or the leader. This kind of internal collapse is very common in the lives of highly frontstage leaders, such as the driven executive who works all the hours he can and is concerned only with his salary and bonus or with rising sales. There comes a time when his personal back stage says, 'Enough!' This may be expressed in the form of a breakdown, physical, mental or emotional; or he may begin to develop unhealthy behaviours backstage that have a destructive life of their own. Leaders who lead only on their front stages burn themselves out, while their followers wither from lack of nourishment, or feel oppressed, or are simply unable to keep up. It was said of Churchill that his generals could scarcely keep up with the pace he set himself relentlessly on his front stage. This kind of leadership can be sustainable in the short term, however, and it may be necessary for a while during a crisis.

Less common is the backstage leader who is unwilling or unable to come onto his front stage. He is less common for one main reason: someone like this will tend not to succeed as a leader. Leadership is necessarily a social enterprise, involving public skills and performance. A leader who finds himself shying away from such encounters and is unable to present himself will struggle in the long run to persuade others to trust and follow him. Any situation in which the leader has retreated backstage for the long term is one in which there will be confusion over authority and a struggle for power, simply because the leader does not occupy the front stage. It is significant how powerful world leaders will do all they can to retain their frontstage presence, even in a personal crisis. Boris Yeltsin managed to make brief public appearances long after his faculties began to fail, Pope John Paul II asked to be propped up in a chair on the balcony of St Peter's Basilica, despite the acute pain and weakness of his last days, because he knew what his visible presence meant to the church. In 2006, Fidel Castro made sure that Cuban TV broadcast footage of him chatting with Hugo Chavez from his hospital bed. Osama bin Laden, too, though long in hiding backstage, has shown that he knows very well the impact of a well-timed appearance on video on al-Jazeera.

Leadership always involves a degree of frontstage 'theatre'. To some extent it is an act put on to convince an audience. Successful leaders are aware of this and set their stage accordingly. They understand the role of context and timing; they appreciate the 'dramatic climax', the appearance of the leader in the hour of triumph. Remember how George W Bush delivered his speech declaring that 'major combat operations in Iraq have ended' wearing pilot's overalls on the flight deck of the aircraft carrier *Abraham Lincoln* (which was steaming in a circle 30 miles off the coast of California at the time). The stage had been set and, when the moment arrived, the leader came on to crown the victory with his presence.

Such 'appearances' on the front stage are all the more significant when a leader has become important as a symbol to her followers. Symbolism is a vital aspect of leadership that every emerging leader needs to appreciate. When someone accepts the role of leader to take a group of people through a difficult challenge, she will always become symbolic in her followers' minds. She comes to represent 'that which will make us safe', a presence that will protect them against an otherwise insuperable enemy. This is an emotional transaction concerned with trust in the face of danger, and when it occurs, people cease to appreciate their leader and relate to her primarily as a person and instead engage with her as a 'sign'.

Symbolization is a powerful mechanism that can work for good or ill, but happens whether or not we choose to acknowledge and welcome it. It is, however, far more dangerous not to acknowledge it, because then a leader cannot choose how to manage it. I suspect that John Paul II understood his status as a symbol and knew that his appearance on the balcony of St Peter's would bring reassurance to anxious souls. He used his presence to soothe. At the same time, he also sought to make his followers aware both of his impending death and of their own attitude to losing him.

This language of 'theatre' and 'performance' will make some leaders a little uneasy. They will feel that it suggests something that is false and lacks the authenticity they believe is essential to leadership. After all, in the first part of this trilogy, *Leading out of Who You Are*, I argued for the moral integrity and authority of the leader at some length. Am I now contradicting myself and advocating that a leader must learn to put on a performance even if it doesn't really represent them as a person? The answer is no. I am not saying for a minute that you should adopt a persona that contradicts your own values. What I am saying is that, at times, a leader chooses to put himself on the front stage in order to deliver a message that underlines the fundamental principles of his leadership, regardless of how he happens to feel at the time. I am saying that being a leader involves a public responsibility: it is not simply a private or personal act. When you accept a role in leadership, you accept a public life in which your behaviour is identified with the institution you represent.

The leader always comes onto the front stage 'in costume'. The costume they wear represents the organization they belong to: it is not their own personal clothing but that of a public body, which they represent to the wider public. In so doing, they accept that they must act on the front stage in accordance with the values, standards and scripts of that body. They are not at liberty to go 'off-script', to fail to come on stage that night or to appear in their own clothes.

The private morality of leaders must be taken seriously by the public bodies they represent. A leader who in his private life breaches trust by evading tax, for example, does not have the right to insist that the employees of his organization shouldn't fiddle the books. A leader who drives to work in a supercharged four-litre sports car doesn't have the right to argue that others in her company must take the bus or cycle to work so that the company can claim it's committed to saving the planet through its corporate transport policy. A leader who flies everywhere when he could 'videoconference' has no right to argue for cuts elsewhere in business travel so that the firm can meet its CO_2 emissions targets. The leader who demands a six-figure bonus for herself has no right to instigate a round of salary freezes or cuts to meet a budget deficit.

If a public body does not have a public line on an issue, I take it that this is an area in which its leaders are free to make their own choices in their personal lives. If there is no obligatory script frontstage, they are at liberty to write their own script backstage. However, if anything is prescribed out front, what the leaders do backstage needs to be congruent with it.

THREE

A Choice of Forces: Strong or Weak?

Arguably, no single figure in the last hundred years represents so clearly the stark choice between strong and weak force as Mahatma Gandhi, the central figure in the story of India's independence. The British had ruled the vast subcontinent since 1858 and were reluctant to give up the jewel of their empire, despite agitation from the early 1900s and actual insurrection from 1919. Gandhi's campaign was unprecedented in that he called for non-violent resistance (sometimes referred to as 'passive resistance' or 'civil disobedience'). Instead of riots, or even warfare, the principles of non-violence committed the rebels not to defend themselves in the face of aggression.

The British response was a classic illustration of the systemic use of strong force. The authorities suppressed peaceful protests brutally with staves, rifle butts and bullets, most notoriously at Amritsar in 1919, when 379 Indians were shot dead and some 1,200 wounded. They maintained control through law enforcement, arrest and imprisonment, and managed the country by bureaucracy, fostering fear rather than trust. Strong force is that which imposes shape and direction in any situation in order to effect an outcome decided by whoever is applying that force.

In contrast, the protesters used a kind of weak force to exert influence. The bonds that bound them to each other were those of belief, not of contract. The determination to resist British rule was based on kinship rather than compulsion. Their chief weapons were respect and courage rather than the baton and the gun. Gandhi and others exercised their leadership through setting an example that inspired trust rather than through legal or military control. Thus the strong force of British rule was ultimately overturned by the weak force of the resistance. There has been no clearer or more challenging demonstration of weak force in action in the political arena, and within a decade it had inspired the Civil Rights movement led by Martin Luther King in America. However, while non-violence is perhaps the most extreme example of the application of weak force, there are many other, less demanding and more domestic examples.

Strong force sets the agenda. It irrupts into a situation and reconfigures the social, emotional or contractual landscape to suit its own requirements. Strong force is morally neutral—it can be used for good or ill, it can set people free or it can enslave and destroy them. It enforces its will, and is often unilateral and decisive. It generates confrontation and competition. It creates winners and losers.

Other examples of the use of strong force might be:

- Pulling a child out of the road when they run out in front of a car
- Attracting an audience when telling a story at a party
- Dominating a discussion in a meeting
- Exercising authority to make a final decision after a debate
- Choosing whether to hire or fire an employee
- Determining the values and standards of behaviour that are acceptable in your home
- 'Casting a vision' that is so compelling that it energizes people
- Selling a product to a customer through your powers of persuasion

In contrast, weak force comes into a situation and respects what it finds there. Often, it forgoes its own, individual success in order to enable the whole group to succeed. Often, it downplays its expertise in order to allow others to shine. It uses its knowledge and strength to empower others and give them confidence. It works by fostering respect, belief and good will. It finds solutions that all parties believe they have a share in. It is responsive, and seeks win-win outcomes. Here are some examples of the use of weak force:

- Submitting to the 'due process' in a democracy that gives each adult one vote
- Reaching a consensus around the meal table about which film the family is going to watch
- Encouraging a pupil to find his own answers by asking him the right questions
- Listening to a patient to enable her to feel 'held', heard and respected
- Building trust and a sense of belonging in a team through open and respectful listening
- Responding to an emergency call, even in the middle of your dinner
- Hitting easy shots on the tennis court so your young daughter can win the point and feel good
- Instigating a corporate listening exercise as chair of the board in order to collect, hear and respond to the views of the workforce

We are familiar with situations that exploit the advantages of both strong and weak force. For example, the 'good cop, bad cop' routine used by interrogators and teachers alike works on this principle. The 'good cop' applies weak force, winning your trust, showing friendship and understanding, making you feel you have an ally you can trust, while the 'bad cop' exerts strong force through threats and sanctions. Your fear of the bad cop makes the appeal of the good cop all the more compelling.

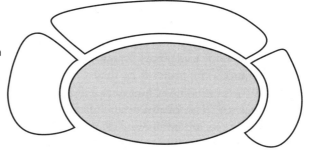

Strong force is that which imposes shape, direction or constraint—eg strong personalities, positional power, formal authority and 'vision casting'.

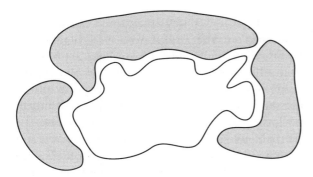

Weak force is that which resources people through affiliation, respect or trust—eg responding to need, creating consensus, fostering trust, offering an invitation and making a sacrifice.

Diagram 3.1: Strong and weak forces in a situation

When I introduce these ideas in seminars, I find that some people feel uncomfortable with the juxtaposition of the words 'weak' and 'force'. They argue that this is surely a contradiction in terms—to be weak is to have little force. Our society has come to associate force, like power, with being strong and dominant, and to associate weakness with being submissive and having no influence. However, we may question this assumption that weakness cannot be forceful and influential.

One way of considering strong and weak force is to think of them in terms of ties or bonds. Strong force creates unilateral ties that give your followers little choice—they are simply overwhelmed by force of argument or personality, the weight of the law or the size of the enemy's army. The relationship between leader and follower is one of imperative: the follower has no choice but to consent and follow. When you yield to strong force you may be doing so against your will, and often it is because it is the least bad of all possible options. Strong force creates ties that may sometimes (though not always) fail to excite the deeper emotions people feel for each other, such as respect, trust, love, affection and compassion. In contrast, weak force relies on all these emotions to create an attachment—the only ties that weak force involves are the free will, desire, hope and belief of the follower. The leader, through her use of weak force, elicits trust from the follower, which is freely given to her in informed consent. In this way, both leader and follower are explicitly, consciously committed to the same outcome.

Weak force often takes longer to exercise than strong force, which is one of the reasons why it is not always suitable in an emergency. You need to move fast when the threats are imminent—the time for reflection comes later, when the crisis has passed. Strong force appears to be dominant and it achieves its ends; but in fact it often happens that resolutions achieved through strong force alone, without the use of weak force as well, do not last.

Consider the political realm. A dictator exercises strong force, using torture and terror to create fear and submission. There is no weak force binding the people to the regime. On the other hand, all kinds of 'weak' ties are forming amongst the oppressed populace. Midnight meetings by candlelight bind people together and a sense of solidarity and mutual commitment emerges as former enemies become united against the tyrant. Bridges are built, hopes are kindled, plans are laid, songs of emancipation are sung. As a result, when finally the people have a chance to muster their own strong force, its power is explosive and the tyrant is overwhelmed. However, often what ensues is a sad consequence of the redistribution of power. The very allies who had been bound together in the shared task of overthrowing a strong ruler now find themselves having to share power. They find that now they can and must exercise legitimate strong force, can and must establish a political system in which different groups are represented, can and must organize the infrastructure of the state, can and must define a common national and political identity. Often, this new way of exercising force is very difficult, as we are seeing at present in Iraq. The 'weak' ties that held the oppressed together under the tyrant have loosened and now have to be made tighter in other ways.

Strong force is indeed seductive, but regimes that are unable to establish proper mechanisms for the flow of weak force remain precarious. The establishing of democracy is the only proven mechanism we have to exercise weak force politically. It enshrines the rights, and also curbs the influence, of each single individual: one person, (only) one vote. It is the political and structural means by which we distribute force equally and create 'weak' ties. Of course, it's imperfect. It does not necessarily create unity or harmony. It offers victory often to the largest minority and can overlook the views of the sizeable majority (unless the system employs proportional representation, which is beset with its own problems of paralysis). It doesn't necessarily create trust or affection, though it does help to prevent domination.

Importantly, strong and weak force can be exercised on both the front and the back stage. Strong force on the front stage is an exercise of might. America classically employs strong force in its foreign policy: it prefers to work alone rather than through the 'weak' agency of the United Nations. It believes (often with good reason) that the UN is ineffectual in providing protection for the global community, especially in the face of crises (couldn't we have predicted that a 'weak' organization such as the UN was going to prove ill-equipped to take quick, decisive action in response to an emergency such as the genocide in Rwanda?). America sees itself as getting things done, and in a culture where results matter it has the evidence to prove the impact it makes on the global stage. The UN is a 'weak', frontstage organization which needs to go through protracted democratic processes that can appear paralysed in the face of provocation.

Interestingly, however, America also uses force on its back stage, behind the political scenes. And there it tends to use not strong but *weak* force. Since the end of the Second World War, it has supported regimes that were opposed to other regimes it regarded as a threat, sometimes by secretly supplying arms, for example, sometimes by giving them intelligence. It supported the *mujahedin* in Afghanistan against the Soviets in the 1980s, and throughout that decade armed the Iraqis to fight the Iranians. It prefers to operate in the international back stage with secret deals and favours, rather than fight all its battles on its front stage with 'strong' military force. In fact, some people might argue that it is because of America's covert backstage pacts in one generation that it is left to deal with frontstage conflicts in the next!

FOUR

A Choice of Forces: Expanding or Consolidating?

In the late summer of 1990, Saddam Hussein ordered a massive build-up of troops on the border with Iraq's southerly neighbour Kuwait. He claimed that it had illegally been drilling for oil diagonally and encroaching beyond its own borders. Perhaps his real reason for wanting to annexe Kuwait, however, was that it would give him access to valuable ports in the Gulf, as well as the possibility of seizing the larger oilfields of Saudi Arabia next door. The invasion of Kuwait precipitated what has come to be known in Britain as the First Gulf War and in America as the First Persian Gulf War. In early 1991, President George H W Bush, having assembled a huge alliance of 28 countries and massed their forces on the Saudi border, ordered the start of Operation Desert Storm. Thus began the campaign that broke the Iraqi army's hold on Kuwait and drove it back to Baghdad.

One of the great controversies at the time was whether the Allies should have prosecuted the war to its logical conclusion and removed Saddam from power altogether. In the light of future events, which ended in the Second Gulf War, many have said that they should. But President Bush would later argue that the cost in lives would have been too great. In 1992, his then Secretary of Defense, Dick Cheney, made the same point: 'I don't think you could have done all of that without significant additional US casualties, and while everybody was tremendously impressed with the low cost of the conflict, for the 146 Americans who were killed in action and for their families it wasn't a cheap war. And the question in my mind is: how many additional American casualties is Saddam worth? And the answer is: not very damned many.'[1]

The choices made by all sides in this sequence of events reflect the choices we make between applying what I call 'Expanding' and 'Consolidating' force. In the first instance, Saddam's invasion of Kuwait was a blatant act of expansionism—pushing beyond the current limits of his territory to occupy ground that did not belong to him. The action of America and its allies in

---

[1] Charles Pope, 'Cheney Changed His View on Iraq', *Seattle Post-Intelligencer*, 29 September 2004

response was equally expansionist: the execution of a war on foreign soil implicitly extended their reach.

However, the purpose of their response was, in fact, consolidation. Chiefly, it was feared by America, Japan and other powers that if Saddam not only annexed the oilfields of Kuwait but also managed to seize the Saudi fields nearby, he would control a large proportion of the world's oil supplies—a situation they deemed too dangerous to risk. That first invasion of Iraq, therefore, was motivated by a desire to prevent the destabilization of the global oil market, and with it the global economy. It was an exercise of consolidating force to restore the status quo ante, which had favoured the allies.

Eventually, Bush faced another choice between expansion and consolidation: should he go on extending the operation and remove Saddam from power altogether, or should he settle for the less costly and less risky outcome of merely liberating Kuwait? Perhaps the likely cost of the expansionist option outweighed the potential gains, as Cheney maintained. You always have to weigh the possible benefits of expansion against the possible costs, and in this case, they were deemed to be simply not worth it. Such is the terrain of a leader's daily choices.

One of a leader's principal tasks is to make such choices. For a CEO, it may be between diversifying her company's products or services and improving what it has been making or doing hitherto. For a government, it may be between welcoming immigrants in the hope that they will contribute to the common wealth and turning them away to protect the privileges enjoyed by the existing population. For a church leader, it may be between changing the way the congregation worships and preserving traditions that have endured for centuries. For a quarterback in a game of American football, it may be between going for the high-risk throw to the wide receiver that might gain fifty yards and settling for the security of the running back, who might just sneak a few extra yards.

Every change involves a degree of risk, and leadership is supremely about choices in the face of risk and the hope of reward. The quarterback may choose to use the running back for the first two downs, knowing there is always third down to come; but he may choose to go for the higher-risk strategy—risking an interception—when on that third down there is less to lose, with eight yards still needed. Conventionally, this is conceived as a balance of risk and reward. Models exist to help decision-makers predict whether the risks involved in a particular deal will be outweighed by the rewards if it works out. Western capitalism has been based on the assumption that growth (just another word for financial expansion) is a good thing if it can be achieved at a low enough cost. Growth in sales figures, growth in corporate profits, growth in a country's gross domestic product—these are all things to which we instinctively aspire in the West. We hear endless news reports celebrating our burgeoning national wealth—or despairing when the figures fall. Growth, expansion, taking more ground, selling more goods, this is what the capitalist machine does. It taps into that basic human drive to possess, control and dominate. Western capitalists—business leaders, politicians, educationalists and the like—have never understood the fundamental idea of communism: that the goal is to share our goods rather than to acquire more of them. The capitalist ideology assumes that it's always better to have a larger pie, even if you get a smallish slice of it, than a smaller pie that is shared out more equally.

Western civilization has been built, since its beginnings in ancient Greece and Rome, on the assumption of the benefits of expansion. The Greeks taught us to aspire to expand our knowledge and our intellectual range, the Romans to aspire to extend our territory and improve our technology. Likewise, the Renaissance taught us to aspire to a richer and more diverse culture, the Enlightenment to aspire to greater freedom and autonomy, the Industrial Revolution to aspire to greater efficiency and productivity. Today, the communications revolution is teaching us to aspire to omniscience and omnipresence. Aspiration lies at the heart of the Western enterprise, an enterprise that has been the engine of the world for the past five hundred years. Aspiration to own more, control more, understand more boils down to the simple, unequivocal belief that expansion is a good. It's better to have more rather than less.

We find ourselves now at a time in history when such assumptions are no longer axiomatic. We no longer accept unlimited expansion as necessarily morally valid, or even materially possible. In the 20th century, people began to question the moral right of imperialists to lay claim to lands not their own, and in due course imperial rule across the world was dismantled and power was given back to the nations and cultures from which it had been taken. We became aware that our expansionist drives were not morally neutral, because they almost always involved taking something from other people. Expansion involves moving into a space you don't currently occupy and claiming it for your own. In the West, we simply assumed our right to do so—the land grab was legitimate. However, territory is rarely unoccupied and just available. Western expansionism has involved a fair amount of theft, and by that I mean more than just complicity in the robbery of the slave trade.

Nor is that theft merely from other peoples whose lands or resources we have taken as our own. We are also stealing from our own children and grandchildren. We are now aware that the legacy of our expansionism is an ecological burden that not we but future generations will have to bear. Whether it is the side-effects of our energy-profligate lifestyles, which are changing the climate of the planet, or the exhaustion of its mineral resources to build and power our transport systems, or the depletion of its soil and water as we farm the earth intensively to feed our growing population, or the extinction of its other species as we invade their habitats. These are footprints we are leaving not primarily on our earth but on the earth of our descendants. It will be they who look back with horror and anger at the way we squandered and destroyed the wealth we should rightly have bequeathed to them.

In short, having been built on the assumption that expansion is good, industrial society now finds itself reaching the limits of the space into which it can expand. In fact, 'space' is now the big issue facing the population of this planet: not as in fanciful notions of colonising Mars, but space here on Earth—how we occupy space. A hundred years ago, there were enough lands uncharted, species undiscovered, sources of mineral wealth untapped to sustain continued exploitation. Now, the end is in sight, and we are only too aware of the finiteness of the system we live in. The Earth and its people are not simply inexhaustible. Resources can run out. And some of those that do can never be replenished.

Expansion is when we extend our territory or possessions—eg developing new ideas, increasing our funds or other resources, enlarging our influence or our social capital

Consolidation is when we stabilize and build up what we already have but could lose—eg deepening trust in relationships, securing our teaching or practices, rehearsing our traditions, caring for the weak and needy

Diagram 4.1: Expanding and consolidating forces

And so a new ethic is beginning to emerge. Previously, business books on leadership extolled the benefits of growth unequivocally, with no thought for the consequences. Those that told you how to double your profit, squeeze your supply chain and exploit the next emerging market opportunity sold by the million. Now, however, those reckless days are coming to an end, and instead a more responsible and (dare I say?) mature counsel is beginning to be heard. The environmental impact of our supply chains and our packaging, the conditions of our labour force, the contribution we are making back to the community are now live issues in the business world, issues that are becoming more urgent by the day. There is a realization that relentless expansion has imposed a cost not only far away in developing countries but here in our own country: it has weakened the bonds and disrupted the rhythms of society, put pressure on families and homes and created a growing underclass. We have shredded the social fabric and now find ourselves engaged in ever more urgent repairs. While our expansionism is not yet dead, we are increasingly appreciating the value of consolidation and the necessity of it.

Expansion and consolidation are not merely alternative business strategies for making the next buck. Those days, we should all hope, are gone. The need for human beings to have goals to aspire to remains as strong as ever; but now those goals need to be reconsidered. As we consume the earth's material resources, the horizons we need to broaden are the non-material ones—horizons of intellectual growth, cultural enrichment, social diversity and spiritual depth. We have grown fat on a rich material diet in the West, but in many other respects we are starved. What we require today is not a business culture in which growth is penalized and executives are risk-averse, but one that sees itself as serving these other human needs—whose meeting in fact consolidates our welfare, protects our health and secures our long-term future on this planet.

Expansionism is always about pushing existing boundaries. It may be reactive or proactive; it may create new circumstances or respond to a demand. It improves performance and delivers more output. Expansionism takes risks by changing things; it doesn't settle for what it already has, it's restless and always wants more efficiency. Examples of expansionist leadership include:

·   Driving business to achieve growth and increased sales
·   Diversifying into new areas of business
·   Caring for more patients by reducing the time you give to each
·   Writing a book full of original ideas
·   Extending your network of relationships to increase your social capital
·   Getting a better performance from your team by offering them performance-related rewards
·   Motivating your team to come up with new and better solutions by taking them away on a retreat

Examples of leadership that consolidates include:

·   Deepening the shared convictions, values and beliefs in a group or organization
·   Giving up a difficult and risky project to avert the possibility of failure
·   Insisting on due process, financial, managerial or whatever, in any organization
·   Stopping on the journey to look after those who are tired or hungry or whose feet are sore
·   Resisting the pressure to reduce the time per patient because that would compromise patient care
·   Establishing a consensus in a group discussion before continuing

FIVE

Combining Forces

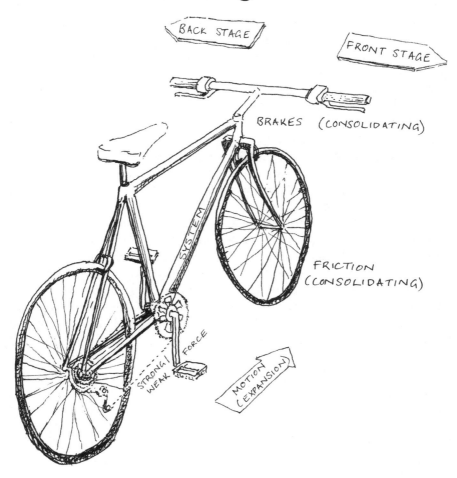

There are, then, three different pairs of forces that can be applied in any situation:

- Frontstage/backstage force
- Strong/weak force
- Expanding/consolidating force

Of course, these forces are not applied in isolation: they are applied in combination, and work in concert with each other. Again, it's rather like the way a cyclist has to apply force to the pedals, the handlebars and the brakes. Turning the handlebars enables her to steer it in the direction she wants to go, and in a similar way a leader has to choose whether to steer towards the front stage or the back stage. Then the cyclist must decide how much force to apply to the pedals. She could pedal as hard as she can all the time, but then she might fall off going round a sharp bend and in any event she would exhaust herself. So, what is needed is the *judicious* use of force. In the same way, a leader cannot apply strong force to his organization all the time without the risk that it will either become exhausted or will lose its balance on more difficult terrain that must be navigated with gentler weak force.

Finally, the cyclist knows when to accelerate and when to use the brake. Both her feet on the pedals and her grip on the brake levers apply force, but their effects are opposite. One speeds the machine up, the other slows it down. Slowing down requires force just as much as speeding up—which is worth noting, as some people equate consolidation with laziness and lack of application. Of course, the bike could be allowed to freewheel and after a time friction will slow it down and bring it to a halt. But the wise leader, too, knows when to accelerate and when to brake.

The cyclist must learn to do all three of these things at the same time and must understand how each relates to the others. Pedalling faster while turning sharply changes the bike's orientation and position rapidly and is a difficult move to master. On the other hand, freewheeling and braking at the same time brings the bike to a gentle standstill, but only if the handlebars are kept upright; to turn sharply would result in a dramatic, possibly catastrophic, loss of balance. The cyclist must use the three forces—pedalling, steering and braking—in concert with each other if she is successfully to navigate the road she is travelling on.

If we think about the three different pairs of forces—frontstage/backstage, strong/weak and expanding/consolidating—we find that there are eight different ways they can be applied in concert. First, there are the four ways that force can be applied through and to the front stage (or what I will call the 'presented' stage, which I abbreviate to P):

Front stage (presented) +	Strong/weak	Expanding/consolidating	Legend
	Strong +	*Consolidating*	*(PSC)*
	Strong +	*Expanding*	*(PSX)*
	Weak +	*Consolidating*	*(PWC)*
	Weak +	*Expanding*	*(PWX)*

Then there are the four ways that force can be applied through and to the back (or 'reserved') stage (which I abbreviate as R):

Back stage (reserved) +	Strong/weak	Expanding/consolidating	Legend
	Strong +	*Consolidating*	*(RSC)*
	Strong +	*Expanding*	*(RSX)*
	Weak +	*Consolidating*	*(RWC)*
	Weak +	*Expanding*	*(RWX)*

These eight combinations represent eight different patterns of power, each with its own character. We can consider their unique properties by building up the descriptions. The chart below presents the kind of characteristics that would be present if (for example) strong and consolidating (SC) forces were combined, and then goes on to show how these would be affected if a leader exerted them on the front stage (P) or the back stage (R). The chart then looks at the combinations strong/expanding (SX), weak/consolidating (WC) and weak/expanding (WX).

Strong/weak with Expanding/consolidating	Frontstage/backstage
SC The combination of strong force and the drive to consolidate means the leadership is concerned with territorial control. Effectiveness, reliability and consistency are the key outcomes. Risk, diversity and ambiguity are reduced in favour of clarity and control.	**PSC** When this combination is applied on the front stage, it creates a *commanding*, authoritative style. Force is used directively to assert control. Disagreement may lead to confrontation, as the leader perceives it as a territorial threat. Followers are required to conform.
	RSC When this combination is applied on the back stage, it creates a *foundational*, enabling style. Force is used to establish solid values, method and practice. The leader establishes clear boundaries, processes and expectations that enable followers to feel secure without being micromanaged.

Strong/weak with Expanding/consolidating	Frontstage/backstage
SX The combination of strong force and the drive to expand means the leadership is concerned with creating the confidence, motivation and means to achieve more. Change, belief, hope and challenge are the key outcomes. Inconsistencies are no longer tolerated and the status quo and accepted norms are rejected in favour of opportunity and growth.	**PSX** When this combination is applied on the front stage, it creates a *pacesetting*, performance-focused style. Force is used directively to generate greater output. Failure to improve performance and attain targets will tend not to be tolerated. Followers are required to show a desire and commitment to excel.
	RSX When this combination is applied on the back stage, it creates a *visionary*, inspirational style. Force is used to capture the imagination, hope and belief of the followers, possibly through vision, passion or personality. The leader challenges their limited horizons, presenting a bigger world into which she can lead them.
WC The combination of weak force and the drive to consolidate means the leadership is concerned with creating space for others to act and ensuring that others take responsibility. Openness and the abilities to listen, accept consensus and tolerate diversity are key outcomes. The associated risks of a lack of centralized control are accepted.	**PWC** When this combination is applied on the front stage, it creates a *consensual*, democratic style. Processes are adopted that allow the collective voice to emerge without being controlled, dominated or manipulated. This social cohesion is the goal of the leadership, which fosters a sense of unity and gives the followers collective responsibility for choice.
	RWC When this combination is applied on the back stage, it creates a *self-emptying*, passive style. The leader allows others to take prominence and follow through their own initiatives, whatever the outcomes. By relinquishing active influence, the leader allows other leaders to emerge and accepts the risks associated with this lack of authority and control.
WX The combination of weak force and the drive to expand means the leadership is concerned with being responsive, reactive and alert to opportunity. Flexibility, fluidity and dynamism are the key outcomes. The leader finds ways to capitalize on the situation that emerges by responding to and adding to its growing momentum.	**PWX** When this combination is applied on the front stage, it creates an *affiliative,* coaching style. The leader fosters a dynamic atmosphere of adventure and mutual belief—'the whole is greater than the sum of the parts.' Central to strategy is that gifts and skills are affirmed and responsibility is delegated—leader and followers alike feel part of a single community with a single goal.
	RWX When this combination is applied on the back stage, it creates a responsive, *serving* style. The leader maintains a low-key presence in the background, working with individuals or small groups to encourage or persuade or solve problems. Like a second in a boxing ring, the leader seeks only to prepare his team for the contest.

We can present this information in the form of a chart that I call the Leadership Strategy model.

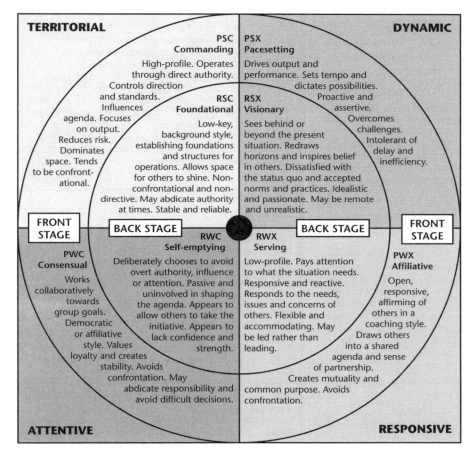

Diagram 5.1: The Leadership Strategy model

These eight different strategies represent the full repertoire of skills that are involved in effective leadership. However, before you can learn to use them all in concert, you need to understand exactly what they do and how and when to use them.

Throughout history, there have been leaders who exemplified one of these strategies in particular. Of course, they all employed other strategies at other times—they were not limited to just the one—but it was perhaps their use of one particular strategy at a particular juncture in history that really marked them out as leaders. I have picked out the following:

RSC: Abraham Lincoln and the Foundational strategy
PSC: Franklin D Roosevelt and the Commanding strategy
PWX: Ronald Reagan and the Affiliative strategy
RWX: Jimmy Carter and the Serving strategy
PSX: Winston Churchill and the Pacesetting strategy
RSX: Martin Luther King and the Visionary strategy
PWC: Nelson Mandela and the Consensual strategy
RWC: Jesus of Nazareth and the Self-emptying strategy

We shall look at each of these in turn in the next few chapters.

PART II

THE EIGHT STRATEGIES OF POWER IN AN ORGANIZATION

SIX

Abraham Lincoln and the Foundational Strategy (RSC)

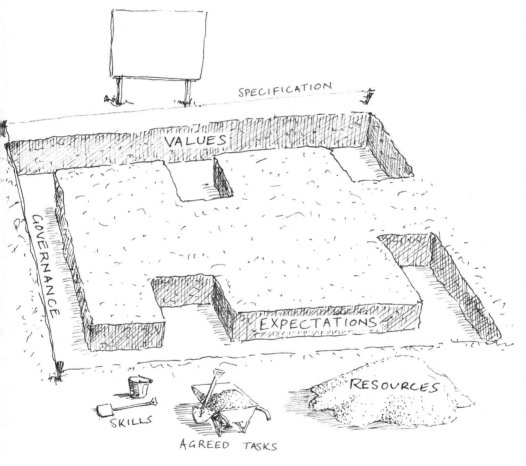

The American Civil War, which began in 1861, was largely predicated on one divisive issue, which threatened the very foundations of the Union. On the one hand, the Northern Yankees regarded slavery as morally repugnant and demanded its abolition; on the other, the Confederates defended the right of the Southern states to make their own choices. At the heart of the bloody struggle that ensued was the tall, angular figure of Abraham Lincoln, the Republican who had been elected president in November 1860. His appeal for the electorate had had much to do with the perceived chaos and corruption in the previous, Democrat administration, which the Republican press portrayed as having sunk the nation into 'a gulf of corruption and misrule'. The times demanded 'moral independence in politics and a new Luther'.[2] In the eyes of many, Lincoln met that need.

He was presented as a man who upheld the doctrines of the Bible as the foundation for all human good. Although he was not in any way a preacher or an evangelist for his faith, Lincoln's stature, style and rhetoric reinforced the quiet but powerful impact of his perspective on life and his fundamental values. What is noteworthy is that, like the German Reformer Martin Luther three centuries before him, who went back to the roots of Christianity, Lincoln constantly appealed to the roots or foundations of the Constitution as the basis of his leadership and his political agenda. For him, the Union was fundamental. 'I hold that in contemplation of universal law and of the Constitution the Union of these States is perpetual,' he argued in his first inaugural address. It was that Union that he believed must exist to bear the weight of all other social and cultural enterprise. Thus he could argue that the Union itself was more essential to him even than the abolition of slavery. In response to an editorial in the *New York Tribune*, he wrote on 22 August 1862: 'I would save the Union. I would save it the shortest way under the Constitution. The sooner the national authority can be restored; the nearer the Union will be "the Union as it was". If there be those who would not save the Union, unless they could at the same time save slavery, I do not agree with them. If there be those who would not save the Union unless they could at the same time destroy slavery, I do not agree with them. My paramount object in this struggle is to save the Union, and is not either to save or to destroy slavery.'

Lincoln understood that no freedom could stand securely except on strong social and political foundations. He believed it would be dangerous (to risk being anachronistic) to play the game without a clear set of agreed rules and a referee to enforce them—such a situation would quickly deteriorate into anarchy. His instinct was for an orderly society in which freedom was made possible by the assumptions shared by all.

His political posture and legacy demonstrate the use and advantages of the RSC strategy in a political arena. The strategy works by applying strong force to the backstage ('reserved') in order to consolidate the situation. For Lincoln,

---

[2] *Cincinnati Gazette*, 26 March 1858; *New York Tribune*, 16 May and 25 June 1860

the Constitution was foundational: the nation would be built on it. Undermine it, and the Union it created, and the entire edifice would become unstable. This foundation didn't dominate the front stage of American life, but without it the American way of life was impossible. Without the clarity of its control and the legal boundaries it set, the freedom that characterized the front stage would have been in jeopardy. Lincoln illustrates the role of the RSC strategy in leadership and the benefits it brings. It is the most basic and most important ingredient in any leadership initiative—without it, the initiative is bound to fail. When a leader employs this strategy, his followers understand what is expected of them in terms of values, standards and practice. This sets the boundaries of acceptable behaviour and the terms of all discussion. Leadership is concerned with creating a stable foundation by establishing underlying values and clear procedures, securing adequate resources, skills and competences and defining good practice.

What the Foundational strategy can achieve

Imagine being in a play for which no rehearsals have been scheduled. The actors turn up when they like and learn their lines if they can find the time. There is no clear guidance from the director, and the lighting team are unpredictable. The wardrobe is badly resourced, and no one can agree on what kind of set is wanted. To act in such a situation would be extremely stressful. In fact, the production would be a shambles. All of these things, the backstage concerns of a theatre, need to be decided, resourced and organized. Otherwise, the frontstage performance becomes chaotic.

When a leader employs the RSC Foundational strategy, she is laying out the backstage area of her theatre of operations: setting in place the agreements, boundaries, rules and expectations. What this does is to make the space 'safe' for the people occupying it. A good example of this at a domestic level is a family routine. Children who grow up in homes where mealtimes and bedtimes are set live in a world that they can predict. Where there are clear guidelines on behaviour, and they know the consequences of misbehaviour, they are able to predict what will happen to them if they choose to do X or Y. This makes children feel safe: they know their boundaries. In contrast, children who lack such social boundaries tend to betray signs of anxiety. They may seek attention or try to take control of a situation in order to make it safer. The 'backstage' foundations provide the stability for children to enjoy freedom on the front stage.

This is rather like the function of rules in sport. It isn't the rules of basketball that the fans turn up to watch—they turn up to watch the game; but in order for there to be a game to watch, the players have to consent to certain behaviours, according to a common code of practice with agreed rewards and penalties. The rules of the game are what gives their interaction on the court both shape and meaning. Everyone agrees to abide by them, and if anyone opts out, it is the game itself that censures them.

Action and reaction

According to Newton's Third Law of Motion, in the physical world every action has an equal and opposite reaction. Social systems are too complex and confused, and involve too many unknown variables, for anyone to try to propose a similar general law governing social actions and reactions. Nonetheless, allowing an inevitable degree of latitude, it is possible to find some reasonably predictable patterns emerging in any social system when social forces are applied. The idea of an *ecology* of power suggests that, if a force is applied to one part of a system, insofar as that system is closed there will be a reaction in another part of it.

...freedom to explore on the front stage.

Strong foundational power backstage underpins...

We have been thinking about the RSC Foundational strategy, which applies a strong force to the back stage to consolidate the situation. What is opposite to the back stage is, of course, the front stage, and this is where you would expect a reaction. Moreover, you would expect it to be opposite in character and direction to the action that provokes it. Accordingly, you would predict that on the front stage the reaction would be weak rather than strong and expanding rather than consolidating. In other words, if an RSC strategy is pursued on the back stage, you would look for a PWX reaction to introduce a weak and expansive force on the front stage.

Consider what tends to happen when an RSC strategy is applied to a social system. For example, if you watch a brilliant soccer team such as Brazil you will notice how they are able to adapt their play depending on the nature of the opposition. They can keep it tight or go wide, play defensively or go all-out in attack. This flexibility is the fruit of hundreds of hours of work on their back stage, the training ground, where skills are honed, communication is developed, moves are learned. Their ability to adapt has not come by chance: it is the product of practice.

Or consider the family that has clear, established boundaries and expectations of behaviour. Because those RSC foundations are in place, the children are free to explore and discover, play and have fun on the front stage, knowing the limits they must remain within. They know that as long as they tidy their bedrooms before bedtime they are free to make as much mess as they want. As long as they are kind to one another, they can play as they like. They know they will be given such-and-such an amount of pocket money on a Friday, and they can then spend it, within reason, on whatever they choose.

The same is true of any organization. If you want your staff to feel trusted and empowered and free from micromanagement, work as hard as you can to establish the goals of the project and your expectations with regard to behaviour and to arrange all the resources that are needed—and then let the staff work with them (and, indeed, improve on them) as best they can. In 2004, the BMW management told the assembly-line workers in its Oxford factory they would like to know of any ways the workers thought the production process could be improved. Over the next few months, more than 500 suggestions were forthcoming, which even extended to enhancing the design of the Mini, the car the factory manufactured. Many of these ideas were acted on and as a result BMW reckoned it saved millions. The company trusted its workers. The management explained what they were trying to do, and the workers understood their goals, their principles and their needs. They were asked to improve on the manufacturing process within those constraints, and they did.

Lincoln's insistence on the Constitution was a crucial turning-point in American political history. It established the Constitution as the basis of American society, and shaped a policy towards slavery that was to bear fruit in emancipation and eventually, after the advent of the Civil Rights movement a hundred years or so later, desegregation. Moreover, it proved that the 'backstage' foundations were strong and broad enough to sustain the changes modern life entailed. Ultimately, it made possible the freedom and security America has enjoyed for more than a century, and its continuing expansion.

Most leadership situations go wrong because the foundations were not properly laid. By the time things break down, it is often too late to do much about it. Like underpinning a house once it has been built, strengthening the foundations of an ill-thought-out project is very difficult once it is under way. This is the current position in Iraq. The lack of any considered strategy to rebuild that society, let alone any consensus on how it should be structured, has plunged the country into chaos and civil war. No one can be safe because that society has no agreed boundaries to hold it together. It matches Emile Durkheim's definition of anomie (literally, lawlessness): the absence in a society of any shared values or morals or other agreements, which rapidly descends into anarchy.

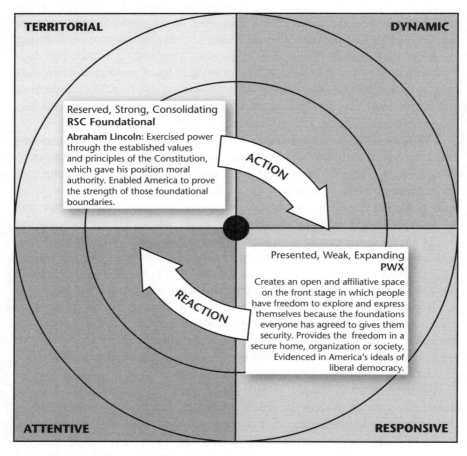

Diagram 6.1: Foundational (RSC) action and PWX reaction

How does a leader implement an RSC strategy?

There are four key elements to implementing this strategy effectively:

1. Establish a culture of ownership and membership at the outset

The essence of RSC is that everyone agrees what they are there to do and how they are going to go about it. The development of shared rules, customs and traditions is critical for any group, organization or society. Not only do they organize life, they create a sense of belonging and membership. The retired British general Sir John Hackett insists that an army relies on such common cultural assumptions: 'Many of the military forms—the worship of regimental totems, eccentricities of dress and customs, the cultivation of the separate identity of the group—these have been developed to the creation and maintenance of that coherence on which the effective performance of a group under pressure depends.'[3]

· Establish what is expected from any activity or project. Why is each person taking part? What does he or she expect to achieve by when? What will they be making available for the project in terms of time, resources, skills and so on?

· Establish the parameters you expect of people. How many meetings will be involved? When will they take place? What is expected from each? How will people communicate and who do they need to keep informed of their progress?

· Establish the shared practices and behaviours that *you* as leader will commit yourself to—for example, always discussing things with the team before making any decision on spending over a specified amount, attending all meetings, always listening when someone else is talking, being kind...

· Make it clear that membership of the team entails both privileges and responsibilities. If anyone chooses to join the team, they are choosing to commit themselves to behave as agreed.

· Offer people the chance to opt out of the agreement at the start if they choose not to commit themselves.

2. Delegate responsibilities clearly

Build up a culture of trust in which people are trained and then trusted to deliver on their responsibilities.

I had been trying to build up Andrew's confidence. He lacked belief in himself as a person and would deny that he had anything to offer. Whenever I reminded him of his talents, he would simply shake his head and explain them away. One day, I became fed up. I was tired and I was losing patience with Andrew's fragile ego, so I changed tack.

'Andrew,' I said, 'I need some help. Badly, in fact. I need you to take this group of visitors around the centre. I should be doing it, but I desperately need to get some work finished. Could you do it for me?' Andrew's eyes widened. 'You want me to take visitors around the centre?'

'Yes, I do. And I think you'd do it fine. I need your help on this one. I can't cope without you.'

---

[3] *Serve to Lead*, British Army officers' manual, p23

At this, his demeanour changed. 'Well, OK, I'll give it a go—if you think I'm up to it.'

Andrew took those visitors round, and he has been taking visitors round ever since. He does it brilliantly—and more besides.

What I learned from that experience was that motivation is not just a matter of encouragement and affirmation: it's about delegation and control. What Andrew responded to was being trusted—trusted by me, the head guy, to do something. He rose to the challenge because I believed in him. He also responded to my need. He had always seen me as strong and capable, and scripted himself as weak and needy. I was the one who had always helped him out; but that only had the effect of disabling him, making him believe that he needed people to help *him* all the time. What he required was a little shove into the swimming pool to discover that he could swim after all.

- Delegate clearly if you want individuals to 'represent' the team in certain situations (for example, on certain committees). Ensure that each one is sufficiently informed and able to speak for the team on those occasions.
- Assign responsibilities to specific individuals. There are various reasons why you might give particular people particular jobs—because they need the practice or because you want to boost their self-esteem or to encourage them to work in partnership with others.
- Provide sufficient resources so that everyone can fulfil the roles they have been given.

3. Enable the group to take responsibility for the behaviour of individuals

I had been asked to lead a sales team whose performance had been tailing off in recent months. Its members were relieved when I arrived—they expected me to come up with some new ideas to boost their figures. I was keen to make a success of it, as it was my first job in the organization. However, as I listened to the team it became clear that they were looking for me to carry them out of the mess. I realized that if I tried to do so, and even if I succeeded, I would be making a rod for my own back: the team would simply rely on me in future to sort out their problems. So, instead of starting new initiatives, I simply let things go on as they were for a few months. I instituted fortnightly review meetings and when my colleagues looked at me to fix their problems, I told them that it was their team and their results and if they wanted to improve them, we'd have to do it together. For a while, things got worse, not better, because nothing actually changed; but I stuck to my message and pushed the problem back to them.

After a few months, they came to me and said, 'Look, we're desperate! We've got to change!' 'Good!' I said. 'Well, let's have a look at what might change.' Then we sat down together and agreed where we had been letting each other down on our responsibilities. We reviewed our strategy and together we came up with a new one. And it succeeded. The key to its success was the fact that the team owned it. They had come up with it, not me. They wanted it—things had got so bad, they had no choice. They got the praise when it worked. The solution involved staying in the mess for a little longer than was comfortable—but in the end it was worth it.

- When an individual fails to meet the agreed standards, push the problem back to the group. Resist the temptation to see it as your personal problem—it isn't, it's a problem for the group. Enable them to choose how to take responsibility for the issue.
- Allow the group to come up with solutions to such problems, rather than feeling you have to solve them yourself.
- Be content to allow messy, inefficient situations to continue until the group solves its own problems. Your task is to continue to confront them with the consequences of their choices. If they opt to leave a situation unresolved, make it clear what the consequences will be (for example, loss of revenue, the breakdown of relationships, even the failure of the project). If they choose to do nothing, they choose to allow these consequences to occur.
- A solution they come up with is always better than one you find for them.

4. Enable people to take individual responsibility for the consequences of their actions

Whenever anyone loses their temper, has a tantrum, sulks or moans, their behaviour is not without consequences—it has an effect on others. Leadership involves getting others to take responsibility for their actions. You might do this by saying something like:

- 'When you did X, it made everyone in the team feel Y.'
- 'The consequence of your outburst was that we weren't able to achieve Z in the meeting.'
- 'Is there anything you need to do to put things right?'

The 'putting right' might take one of many forms: writing an apology, seeing and speaking to someone who has been hurt, making up for lost time in their own hours, fixing whatever has been broken. Usually, accepting the consequences involves facing those who have been affected—and, often, asking them what they would like to say about it.

Some examples of RSC leadership in action

- A teacher establishing an agreed set of appropriate values and behaviours for the class
- A corporate health-and-safety policy governing good practice
- A job description that sets out what is expected of the post-holder
- A list, pinned to the fridge, of family rules such as 'Be kind,' 'Take responsibility' and 'Always listen'
- A regular team-meeting that gives rhythm to the week and provides a formal mechanism for feedback
- A set of values and behaviours underpinning a 'citizens' charter'
- A shared set of values and beliefs that bind a religious community together
- A shared story that informs and helps to define the boundaries of a tradition, community or country

When to use an RSC strategy

This strategy is most effective if it's used right from the outset of any endeavour. You wouldn't build a house without laying solid foundations first, and in the same way a leader should not start building her project, team or organization (or anything else) until she has established its foundations. This is especially important when a task is very complex and people may have different expectations.

- When you are setting up a new department
- When there is confusion and uncertainty in the group
- When the team have become disunited or are underperforming
- When you are working with a high-powered team that would react badly to being micromanaged
- When you are moving from the vision or initiation stage of a new enterprise to a period of more settled, efficient productivity
- As a basic, background strategy that you run all the time in 'maintenance mode'

SEVEN

Franklin D Roosevelt and the Commanding Strategy (PSC)

When Franklin Delano Roosevelt was elected president in 1933, he took the helm of a country crippled by the Great Depression. A quarter of the workforce was unemployed. Industrial production had dropped by more than half since 1929. Farming was on its knees, as prices fell by 60 per cent. In a country with limited government-funded social services outside the cities, two million people were homeless. The banking system had collapsed completely. Into this crisis stepped a man who would shape the economics of the next two decades and, arguably, start an engine that has not stopped to this day.

Roosevelt's response to a dire situation was to intervene: to take responsibility and take action. He began his term with an attack on the greed of the private sector, which he saw as a critical element in the recession. In an early address, he delivered this verdict: 'Primarily this is because rulers of the exchange of mankind's goods have failed through their own stubbornness and their own incompetence, have admitted their failure, and have abdicated. ... The money changers have fled from their high seats in the temple of our civilization. We may now restore that temple to the ancient truths. The measure of the restoration lies in the extent to which we apply social values more noble than mere monetary profit.'

His action took the form of the two 'New Deals' between 1934 and 1937. These involved government initiatives to employ young men and enforce codes of practice on industry that reduced competition and encouraged opportunity and reward for the whole workforce. They promoted recovery by 'pump-priming'—injecting $3.3 billion of federal money into the economy and creating the largest government-owned industrial enterprise in American history, the Tennessee Valley Authority (TVA), which built dams and power stations, controlled flooding and modernized agriculture and living conditions in the poverty-stricken Tennessee Valley. Roosevelt also cut costs, slashing the regular federal budget. He cut by 40 per cent the benefits received by veterans, and removed half a million veterans and war widows from the pension rolls. Protests erupted, led by the Veterans of Foreign Wars, but Roosevelt held his ground. He succeeded in cutting federal salaries and reducing spending on research and education, the Army and the Navy.

The situation was so bad that only an imposition from above of a draconian regime could arrest the decline. As it happened, the industrial engine that Roosevelt had started was about to begin firing on all cylinders when the Second World War broke out. The German advance through Poland, Belgium and France was unstoppable, and the Wehrmacht was soon poised for an invasion of Britain. Only 26 miles of water stood between Hitler and total domination of Europe. Britain desperately needed supplies, both military and civil, and Winston Churchill had long been urging Roosevelt to join the war against the Nazis. Roosevelt was to resist until the attack on Pearl Harbor in December 1941, but already a series of addresses to the nation (his 'fireside chats') had prepared the way for 'lend-lease', whereby America's industrial machine was directed to the production of weapons, munitions and other supplies for loan or lease to its European allies. 'We Americans are vitally concerned in your defence of freedom. We are putting forth our energies, our resources, and our organizing powers to give you the strength to regain and maintain a free world. We shall send you, in ever-increasing numbers, ships, planes, tanks, guns. That is our purpose and our pledge.'[4] When Germany invaded the Soviet Union in June 1941, Roosevelt extended lend-lease to the Soviets.

Roosevelt was shrewd in his response to the situation, for he knew that not only would lend-lease generate employment immediately, it would pay dividends in the future, ensuring that America's economy was best placed to prosper after the war. As he put it: 'What we send abroad we shall be repaid, repaid within a reasonable time following the close of hostilities, repaid in similar materials, or at our option in other goods of many kinds which they can produce and which we need.'[5] The military build-up duly generated nationwide prosperity and the number of Americans out of work fell below a million.

Roosevelt's instinctive leadership strategy was a frontstage one: from the outset, he took on the opposition—in this case, business. He demonstrates the role of the PSC strategy, and the benefits it brings. This strategy involves taking control of the situation around you through direct authority. In terms of power, it is the application of force in order to reduce risk and limit diversity and impose order on a chaotic or problematic situation. The leader metaphorically 'fills the space', both with his personality and with the initiatives he sets up. It is the impact a headmaster may have on schoolchildren who are called into his office, or a policeman may have when he arrives on a scene of unrest: both of them have the positional authority and power to impose order and take control. They have the means—including even physical means—to confront and subdue opposition. They act with authority vested in them by an institution or state and convey by the way they stand, the way they walk, the way they talk, that they expect to be obeyed. In their presence, you are immediately aware that the position of authority on the front stage is now filled and that it can only be taken from them by confrontation or subversion.

In 1933, a year of desperate economic crisis, what America needed was just such a figure of authority. Roosevelt took that role, and put in place a centralized system of reforms to drive the economy back towards growth. He was not afraid to intervene from above, to dictate a way forward. The fact that the nation accepted his leadership was much to do with the dire circumstances it found itself in. Much the same could be said of Margaret Thatcher when she hit her stride in the Eighties as Conservative Prime Minister. Britain was in the grip of strikes that were paralysing enterprise and strangling the economy. Thatcher approached her office with the same attitude and mentality as Roosevelt, willing

---

[4] From 'An Arsenal for Democracy', the first of the *Fireside Chats*
[5] Ibid.

to take the opposition on. In both cases, it was an act of confrontation—like a new teacher putting his foot down with an unruly class of children, imposing order and demanding compliance with his rules.

This is one of the key benefits of the Commanding strategy: where disorder is rife, and even fear, it brings order and control. When people feel unsafe, when they have no sense of any boundaries, they need Commanding leadership. PSC is concerned with ensuring that followers know that the leadership 'space' is inhabited and that there are very clear expectations regarding standards of behaviour and practice which will be defended against any challenge. Discussion is always seen in territorial terms and is therefore often confrontational. The leader uses his influence to establish territorial control through forceful authority and clear channels of command. Effectiveness, reliability, consistency and efficiency in delivery are key outcomes. Risk, diversity and ambiguity are reduced in favour of clarity and control.

Such powerful, direct, commanding leadership is often understood in the armed forces to be almost the *only* kind of leadership there is. Every cadet in the British Army receives a copy of a slim, red hardback entitled *Serve to Lead*. In it, the collected wisdom of the Army's great leaders of the past is offered to aspiring young officers. Bernard Montgomery was perhaps the most effective and celebrated military commander in the Second World War, and his campaigns, against Erwin Rommel in the desert of North Africa and later in northern France, were hugely significant in the defeat of the Nazis. This is what he wrote: 'A leader has to learn to dominate events which surround him; he must never let these events get the better of him; he must always be on top of his job and be prepared to accept responsibility.'[6] He suggests that the only appropriate posture for the military leader is domination, the subduing of all around him. For him, a leader who is overtaken by events, who is caught unawares, who loses control, is dangerously negligent. This kind of domination requires of a leader a certain mentality: they must be able to show 'calmness in crisis and decision in action'. Their self-control is such that when crises occur they themselves are composed, measured and focused, and in the heat of battle, with the smell of cordite in their nostrils and the frenzy of combat all around them, they remain clear-thinking and decisive.

Of course, the context for such leadership is primarily one of fear. 'All men are afraid at one time or another,' stated Montgomery. The emotion of fear is not found only on the battlefield, but it is certainly at its strongest in that arena. Safety is the most basic human need—more basic than food or company or love. If you feel that you are threatened, your first act, before anything else, is to try to make yourself safe. You don't sit down for a meal or worry

---

[6] *Serve to Lead*, p21

about being lonely or unpopular when you are in danger. These other needs matter, but not at that moment. And it is for this reason that the emotional response to danger—that of fear—is the most dramatic and compelling of all emotional responses. When the 'fear centres' of the brain, in the region called the 'amygdala', are stimulated, a cascade of hormonal reactions are triggered. Adrenaline and cortisol flood the blood system, flowing round the body and priming it for instant action. The pupils dilate, the pulse quickens, the hands sweat as the body prepares for fight or flight. Self-preservation is the one goal to which all its systems are directed at this moment.

All of us have experienced such physical reactions, no doubt. They may not have occurred in response to a life-threatening situation—it may have been simply during a heated argument, or on a dark night walking home alone, or before a sports match. However, any situation in which control seems to have been lost can feel threatening and can provoke the same kinds of response. The depression of the 1930s was just such a time, when the feeling of fear—for livelihoods, for homes, for futures, for children—was heightened and at times came close to panic. In such situations, what we need is for that fear to be contained. Fear can either be destructive, leading to panic or paralysis, or it can be channelled to produce extraordinary strength and speed of thought and a willingness to sacrifice your less fundamental needs in the greater cause of survival. The effect of adrenaline on the body is to prepare us for action, for our 'fear conditioning system' has evolved to maximize our chance of survival. There can be no better situation for the leader using the PSC strategy to release the very finest performances from those around her.

What the Commanding strategy can achieve

Fear must be channelled, and the key to channelling fear productively is containment. When a small child is frightened, he feels that the world may overwhelm him and he needs to know that there is someone who can stay with him who is bigger than the crisis, big enough not to be overwhelmed. Such a person will act like a container for his fear, preventing it from escaping into unmanaged panic. The calm, strong authority of an adult, the assurance that they know what is going on, that while they, too, may be afraid, they are not panicking—these are the signals that reassure the child that he is not about to be overwhelmed, and contain his fear.

Much the same is required of a leader in a crisis. Her task is to contain and manage people's fear, by being 'big enough' to stay in the situation and show that she herself is not overwhelmed by it. This is the leadership that Montgomery and others call for on the battlefield; but there are all kinds of other situations where this kind of leadership is essential. The brain surgeon needs to exude this kind of authority in the theatre. It would be no good if he started a discussion about the methodology of surgery just as his assistant was about to slice through a major artery! Moreover, it would be disastrous if he allowed poor-quality colleagues to work with him in order to give them a chance to experiment if it meant a threat to the patient. It would be catastrophic if he allowed his team to be lax about hygiene because he didn't want to be dictatorial but wanted to make room for freedom and diversity. Likewise, if you are walking down the road and you see a small child run out in front of a car, you impose PSC leadership on the situation—you grab him and drag him back to safety. This is not the time to start a discussion with him about road safety, or to allow him to take responsibility for his actions!

There are times in life when immediate control is needed, in order to manage and contain fear and danger. There are times when commanding, PSC leadership that 'fills the space' and dominates all around is the only appropriate strategy and not to use it would be a dereliction of duty. However, there are also less immediately critical situations in which the dynamics of PSC leadership are needed. For example, imagine you go for a job interview. You're nervous and keen to impress. But the interview process is shambolic: you weren't told what you should have prepared, no one on the panel introduces themself and it isn't clear who is in charge or how the decision is going to be made. You spend the whole time feeling anxious and uncertain, as the lack of explicit PSC authority leaves you insecure and at a loss. None of your fear is contained: instead, it swills around inside you, making you more and more apprehensive and unsure. You underperform because you try to take some control yourself, and as a result come across as a dominating person.

Now cast your mind back to your first day at school. Your mum takes you in, you find your new classroom and she hands you over to your teacher, who greets you by name (she's obviously learned it) and shows you to your desk (she's obviously prepared it and labelled it). Once everyone has arrived, she stands in front of the class and explains how school works and what's going to happen next. She always waits until there is quiet before she speaks, and then she speaks clearly and calmly. Your first day at school, which is traumatic enough as it is, is made manageable by the strong, clear, calm authority of the teacher. Your anxiety is contained by her reassuring presence. You sense that she is in control and you are safe with her; you feel that, though the situation is frightening, it's not overwhelming. You can cope because you are held together by someone else's authority.

Life is full of little situations like that, where people feel insecure and anxious: at the start of a project, when you are introducing a change in strategy, welcoming new team members, managing uncertainty. In all those situations, the anxiety of the followers needs to be contained by the authority of the leader.

When this strategy is not used in such situations, anxiety rises and what results is a power bid: people sense that there is a leadership vacuum and, to get a grip on the situation, someone or some group will start to exert control. The likelihood is that this will be improper and illegitimate, but in part it happens because there has previously been a failure to contain emotions appropriately. Fear is a powerful emotion, and there are those who will exploit it and those who will run from it. The leader's role is to manage it.

For the past two decades, the credibility of commanding leadership like this has taken a bit of a battering. Accusations of being authoritarian, directive, bullying and even abusive have made people wary of this kind of strategy. The advent of feminism and the growing number of women in leadership have made a previously male-dominated environment more sensitive about some of the more extreme expressions of masculinity. Many men in leadership feel somewhat confused about how to exercise authority without being seen as domineering. At the same time, the language of servant leadership, coined by Robert K Greenleaf in 1970, has encouraged leaders to see themselves in a submissive posture, preferring collaborative and consensual approaches to directive ones.

Many, indeed, would say that the revolution has not gone far enough. They point to continuing examples of bullying, discrimination and executive abuse of authority to show that power is still being used inappropriately. Some thinkers go as far as to dismiss leadership altogether, labelling it 'male patriarchy'. They often make the broad generalization that women do not use power in this way and are basically more collaborative and less dominating. They argue that leadership should eschew power, and that power itself lies at the root of the problems organizations encounter.

Whether or not women are indeed more collaborative and less dominating is beside the point (though I happen to think that, on the whole, they are). What matters to me as a leader, rather than as a male or female leader, is being able to use the right kind of power at the right time on the right occasion. It is absurd to suggest that power itself is the root of the problem. The root of the problem is not power but the *misuse* of power—its incorrect application. This debate has had the unfortunate effect of distracting us from the proper question, which is: How should you *use* power? It has also tended to deny permission altogether for the use of directive force. What I want to help you to understand is that in certain circumstances the use of PSC power is appropriate and, indeed, vital. In fact, not to use in such circumstances would be an abdication of responsibility.

The basic rule for when to use the Commanding strategy is this: when the consequence of *not* intervening would be dangerous if not catastrophic, then is the time to use it. So, for the brain surgeon not to use a PSC strategy in surgery could be fatal, and would be a dereliction of duty. To allow the toddler to run into the path of a car for fear of intervening in a directive way would be absurd and appallingly perverse. This is why such PSC leadership is appropriate in much of military life, where you are dealing often with life-or-death situations. It is also why military institutions schooled in this kind of power from the beginning struggle to adjust to more civilian peacekeeping roles that require the exercise of other kinds of power.

The reaction to the action

One of the reasons for the bad press for the PSC strategy is that often it has been the only strategy a leader, organization or society has exercised. One thinks, for example, of totalitarian regimes, Fascist, Communist or theocratic. In each such case, PSC power is virtually the only kind of power in the system. Or of a feudal system, in which the landowner dominates the peasant farmers. Or of a domineering parent, who crushes his children's freedom to grow up. Or of a bullying executive, who refuses to listen to feedback and defies all challenges to her authority. The result is always the same: the only 'space' available to the followers under such domination is on the other side of the ecology of power, in the Serving posture of RWX. There is no room to compete on the front stage, so the followers retreat to the back. There is no way to exert strong power, unless they stage a coup; so instead the followers are compelled either to be submissive or to find ways of evading the authority and being subversive.

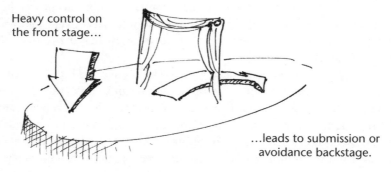

Heavy control on the front stage...

...leads to submission or avoidance backstage.

When they are continually dominated by PSC Commanding power, followers are forced to yield to its demands. The front stage is filled with a strong presence that insists on submission. In reality, it insists that followers must be servants. The RWX Serving posture is the opposite to the PSC posture, and in the ecology of power is the natural response to such domineering authority. Over the long term, the effects are always negative. On the one hand, domination can breed a kind of broken servility, as it did amongst African Americans; a diminished, dehumanized spirit, a lack of self-respect, dignity and regard bred in by decades if not centuries of serving another man's needs. Such use of power is never justified. Those of us who believe that to be human is to be created in the image of God are glad of the courage of those fellow Christians who, armed with the same conviction, fought against the slave trade in the 18th and 19th centuries.

It isn't only in political leadership that such a use of PSC power is unhealthy. The story of Enron illustrates the corrosive effect it can have when it is part of the culture of a corporation. Enron was committed to dominating the market, a strategy that ultimately led its leadership into a dangerous spiral in which, each quarter, it had to undertake more and more devious financial deceptions in order to create the illusion of billions of dollars in profits when the company was actually losing money. This drove up its share price to record levels—at which point, its executives began illegally trading millions of dollars' worth of Enron stock. These insiders knew about the offshore accounts that were hiding the company's losses, but other investors did not. It was a gross example of the abuse of power. Enron executives treated the company's shareholders and its other employees as pawns they could use to their own ends, much as a dictator controls and manipulates a populace without any regard for its welfare. Enron's European operations filed for bankruptcy on 30 November 2001, and Enron itself sought Chapter 11 protection in America two days later. At the time it was the biggest bankruptcy in American history, and it cost 4,000 people their jobs.

Not only does PSC power over the long term often result in a crippling servility, but in the end it can also provoke revolt. Marx was right in his diagnosis that the dominance of the bourgeoisie was unbalanced and would one day precipitate revolution. However, he was wrong in believing that this would inevitably lead to a more stable, egalitarian system. History testifies otherwise. Those who have been dominated and oppressed rarely seek to establish a more equitable system once they come to power. Instead, their experiences under the yoke seem often to foster in them a desire to impose the yoke on others. It seems as if the memories of subjugation and suffering are not so easily erased from the consciousness of the newly empowered. It is the same reason why people who were abused as children often (though not always) go on to abuse as adults; why power-sharing in Northern Ireland has proved so difficult and so unstable since the paramilitaries laid aside their weapons; why Robert Mugabe's regime in Zimbabwe has become increasingly violent and oppressive towards white landowners; and why the more supremacist end of the Black Power movement in America was such an appealing alternative to the civil rights movement in the 1960s.

In most cases, it takes monumental leadership, convinced of the need for generosity and forgiveness, as well as (usually) considerable assistance to establish proper structures of governance, to help people who have been subjugated to make the transition to a more equitable and empowered life without resorting to violence.

The PSC Commanding strategy has, throughout history, been the primary form of power that has ruled countries, organizations and families. The realization in the past 50-odd years that it has often been oppressive is something we should rejoice at. However, it would be a mistake to reject it altogether. It remains a vital application of power that must be available to us if we are to exercise authority properly and develop societies and organizations that are free from fear.

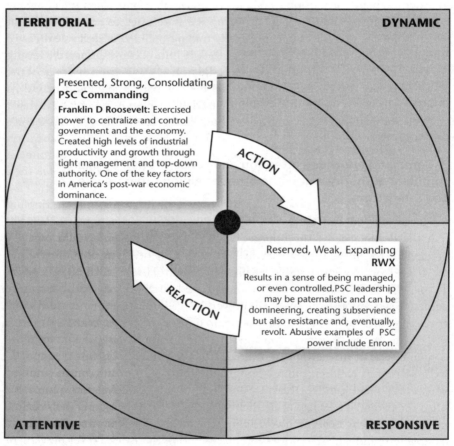

Diagram 7.1: Commanding (PSC) action and RWX reaction

How does a leader implement a PSC strategy?

There are four key elements to implementing this strategy effectively:

1. Establish your presence

- Be at team meetings first so that when others come in you are ready to greet them, rather than looking for something, preparing your notes etc. This is a powerful way of 'shaping the space'. It sets you apart as the secure leader and sets the tone for every session.
- Stand up, straight and tall, make eye contact, smile and look secure and confident.

One of Roosevelt's characteristics was a certain paternalism. His criticism of business was like a father's rebuke to sons who should have known better and were now being called back into line. The forceful 'fireside chats' whereby he coaxed Americans into supporting their country's involvement in the Second World War likewise brought to mind a father teaching his children what was the right decision to make. Arguably, Americans wanted a father figure at the time to rescue them from the mess they were in, as well as to protect them from other, abusive authorities.

2. Command undivided attention and concentration by exuding confident authority, but without undermining other people's dignity and self-esteem

- When introducing any idea at a meeting, dominate the space by ensuring that all eyes are focused on you. Don't begin until they are. You can develop different tactics to achieve this, which may include standing in silence looking straight ahead, reminding the team of the agreement they made always to listen.
- Thank people for their attention in advance, because you expect to receive it!

3. Take unilateral control of a situation when you need to create stability

- When confronted with a volatile or escalating situation, it is your responsibility to take control and re-establish security.
- Deal with the situation through direct presence rather than by e-mail or phone.
- Be more than usually visible during this time, to reassure the rest of the team
- 'Think ahead and don't waste time' (*Serve to Lead*, p26)

4. Engender trust through 'warm' authority when dealing with conflicts

- When possible, get the two sides together in the same room and negotiate between them. Greet each individual with a handshake and a warm smile when they come into the room (you are there first, of course—it's your space they are coming into!). Remember that people will be coming through the door 'emotionally charged'. By receiving them with warmth but also with a sense of formality and professionalism, you are setting the right tone. Hold eye contact, sit up with your shoulders back and talk slowly, clearly and calmly.
- Being authoritative need not make you detached, hard and 'closed'. Warm authority is about having the confidence to be empathetic without losing your objectivity. This means you can say things such as 'I can hear that you're very frustrated,' 'I understand why you're upset' and 'I can relate to your anxiety.'
- Listen carefully to what each person says and ask them if you can repeat it back to them to ensure that you have understood their meaning. This will ensure that they feel heard and that you understand what they are saying and are not misinterpreting it.
- Enable everyone concerned to take responsibility for their behaviour and its consequences. This involves ensuring that they answer two questions:
    What am I responsible for in this situation?
    What do I need to do about it now to put it right? (This could include an apology, a change of behaviour, restitution...)

Some examples of PSC leadership in action

- An executive demanding a 10-per-cent reduction in costs from his board of directors in the next quarter
- A teacher correcting mistakes of spelling and grammar in a student's work
- A parent disciplining a child with a strong 'No!' and immediate repercussions if he transgresses
- A law court passing judgement on a criminal and sentencing him to a term in jail
- A parent strapping a toddler into a buggy
- An officer carrying out a battle plan as directly and effectively as possible

- A consultant surgeon organizing and managing his team in order to perform a safe, effective operation

When to use a PSC strategy

- Always when starting a meeting or a new project, to create reassurance and confidence before moving on to the RSC Foundational strategy to set out the boundaries, expectations etc
- When people are anxious or uneasy
- When there is conflict and you are determining the context in which to bring the two sides together
- When the consequences of not intervening immediately and decisively could be catastrophic (for example, to prevent an accident or a fight)
- When dealing with bullying or with dangerous or immoral behaviour
- When required to attain strategic goals as efficiently as possible

EIGHT

Ronald Reagan and the Affiliative Strategy (PWX)

Ronald Reagan was the 40th president of America. Elected at the age of 69 in 1981, he was the oldest person to hold that office. 'The Great Communicator', as he was called by some, was celebrated for his ability to express ideas and feelings in an almost personal manner, even when delivering state addresses. These were skills he developed in his early career as a movie actor, when he was sometimes compared to the gun-slinging John Wayne. He moved from acting to radio hosting and live television; the rhetoric of politics followed later. As President, Reagan showed that he clearly understood the importance of style in communication and knew that he needed to make an emotional connection with his audience—two lessons he had learned in Hollywood. He hired skilled speechwriters who could capture his folksy charm and he varied his rhetoric according to who he was addressing. He used strong, even ideological, language to condemn the Soviet Union and Communism, but could also invoke a lofty and idealistic vision of America as a defender of liberty.

Arguably, it was Reagan's humour—and especially his one-liners—that most disarmed his opponents and endeared him to the public. During the 1984 campaign, discussion of his advanced years led him to quip in his second debate with Walter Mondale, 'I will not make age an issue of this campaign. I am not going to exploit, for political purposes, my opponent's youth and inexperience.' His opponents and supporters alike noted his 'sunny optimism'. A frequent complaint by his critics was that his personal charm allowed him to say almost anything and still win, a quality that earned him the nickname 'the Teflon President'.

Reagan's positive outlook, his broad, movie-star shoulders and his slightly heroic and romanticized image appealed to a public who wanted to feel better about themselves. The Eighties began with America watching with growing unease the lengthening shadow of Soviet threat: its enemies appeared to be winning the arms race and at the time it wasn't at all clear who would win the Cold War. Nonetheless, Reagan was the first world leader to suggest, in 1983, that Communism was nothing but another bizarre chapter in human history and it would soon come to an end. To hasten this outcome, he built up spending on defence once again, aiming to bankrupt the Soviets if they tried to keep pace. He trusted in the power of capitalism to outperform the Communist machine, and after the anxious smile of Jimmy Carter his confidence was attractive to many Americans, as it reassured them that their country was strong and its prospects good. Perhaps he appealed to something buried in the national psyche—the belief in the potential for growth, the brighter day yet to dawn, the upward curve of the future. Without putting it explicitly into words, his emotional posture epitomized the American Dream, an almost unconscious sense that a better life was available to all.

At an emotional level, Reagan classically exploited the PWX Affiliative strategy. This focuses on the front stage but, in contrast to the PSC Commanding strategy, primarily exerts weak force, appealing to people's need, hope and trust rather than compelling them through obligation or force of will. Also, instead of seeking to consolidate his situation, this kind of leader is expansive, tuning in to its energy and hopes for the future and amplifying them. Being Affiliative is about winning hearts and minds, about finding that emotional resonance with your audience that has them captivated.

This is a subtle business. The finest exponents of this strategy are adept at reading what their audience wants to hear and how it wants to hear it. They are attuned to the transaction going on between them, the principal actor on the stage, and their audience, whose attention they know they must win. Like any actor, they understand that their performance is sustained by the audience, and if the theatre were to empty, the show would come to an end. Leadership involves finding the right style—and the right lines—to keep a possibly fickle audience enthralled. Reagan's performance was one a somewhat tense and fragile nation wanted to see. They wanted to believe in a strong, dominant, warm and kindly figure who was leading them towards a more benign world order. The style Reagan used on the political stage resembled the one he had used in the movies. Many commentators would say that Tony Blair has a similar ability as a leader. He tunes in to the public mood (with the help of focus groups and other market research, of course) and then adopts a position that resonates with 'where people are at'.

In economic terms, Reagan wanted to foster the growth of the free market by reducing the size and scope of government and encouraging enterprise. In 1954, he had regarded Roosevelt's 'New Deal' as 'approaching fascism'. As his former speech-writer Peggy Noonan suggests, 'Reagan had a libertarian conviction, that power is best and most justly wielded from the individual to the community to the state and then the Federal Government—and not from the Federal Government on down. He thought, as Jefferson said, that that government governs best that governs least. He wanted to shrink the bloated monster; he wanted to cut very seriously the amount of money the monster took from the citizenry each year in taxes.' Reagan was sceptical about the ability of the federal government to deal with problems, particularly economic ones. His solution was to reduce its role in planning and control by cutting taxation and regulation in order to allow the allegedly self-correcting mechanism of the free market to operate. On the day of his first inauguration, he said: 'Government is not the solution to our problem; government is the problem.'

Of course, such a message appeals. It sounds good to the hard-working store-owner who is motivated to expand his business if he knows that half his profits will not be taken by the government. This is classic PWX politics—creating freedom on the front stage rather than restricting it, encouraging growth and spending rather than prudence and saving. Many people give credit to Reagan for restoring optimism to a nation that in 1980 was in deep malaise and for advocating a freer rein for the private sector rather than greater government control. Perhaps his hostility to Communism was rooted in his suspicion of any system imposed from the top down rather than arising out of human freedom, ambition and desire.

What the Affiliative strategy can achieve

PWX leadership always looks for ways to motivate rather than restrict people. It is no coincidence that Reagan had previously been a motivational speaker: he understood what people needed to bring out the best in them. The past two decades, since his presidency in the Eighties, have seen the 'motivational industry' swell to colossal size. Organizations pay huge sums for coaches who promise to improve the performance of a team. The psychology of the Eighties was grounded in the feel-good factor of growth, the optimism that arises from the realistic hope that you may acquire more than you currently own. It tapped into raw aspiration. One of the differences between that heady climate of free-market growth in the Eighties and the mood today is the growing awareness that the boom cannot be sustained. Not only have stock crashes come and gone, not only have we lived through 1989's Black Monday and the 'dot-com' boom and bust of the following decade, not only are we more sensitive to the inevitable, predictable cycles of growth and decline in any market, we are also aware now that the entire global system is reaching its limits. The current talk of sustainability and renewability is in marked contrast to that of expansion and acquisition in the late Eighties.

A lot of thinking on leadership over the past two decades has emphasized the role of leader as motivator and visionary, the one who has big, exciting ideas and is able to inspire her staff to work harder to achieve their dreams. Those firms in which the rewards the employees receive are in line with the success of the business are held up as models of excellence. As we have become more suspicious of the directive approaches of the Commanding strategy, so we have favoured this more Affiliative, coaching style, in which the leader comes alongside us. Her language is of 'us' and 'we' as opposed to 'you' and 'I'; her tone is not demanding, not hectoring, but understanding, appealing and encouraging. Her message is 'I know where you are at present and I sense that together we can get to a better place in the future.' We see her as one of us, but also as someone who busily goes around keeping our spirits up, believing always in the brighter day to come.

There is no doubt that, in the sweep of history, such optimistic affirmation made a welcome change from the somewhat dour, puritanical style of much of the first half of the 20th century. Replacing duty with freedom and grim obligation with the energy of hope released Western society from some of its more repressive behaviours. It cultivated personal expression, individual liberty and human rights, while opposing the centralizing influences of government and other institutions. It encouraged us to look forward rather than back and fostered a generation of 'boomers' who have exploited (and, arguably, squandered) the opportunities of post-war society in their pursuit of individual happiness. The psychologies of our day endlessly repeat their mantras of 'releasing your potential', 'achieving personal fulfilment', 'unblocking your obstacles to growth' and 'moving from good to great'.

There are, however, three pitfalls into which such a message can lead us unless we are careful. The first is that assurances of a rosy and expansive future may simply be false. Relentless optimism does not itself make our prospects better. Nor does the urge to bury bad stories in the press and put a positive spin on events help us to grow up and take responsibility. Second, the leader can end up being more pal than boss. If you are just 'one of the boys' and can't stand apart, you quickly lose authority, respect and control. Third, the PWX message of fulfilment may ultimately be little more than straightforward, old-fashioned selfishness. The term 'selfish' itself sounds rather quaint to our ears, being reminiscent of the narrow-minded post-war restrictiveness of our parents' and grandparents' generations, and by replacing the idea of selfishness with 'self-fulfilment' we have whitewashed the negative connotations of self-orientated activity.

Appropriate and healthy Affiliative leadership is a subtly but significantly different matter from merely appealing to 'personal growth'. For a start, it is communitarian rather than individualistic. The PWX leader appeals to 'us', not 'me'. The picture she paints is of the group setting out on the journey together, where the happiness, freedom and fulfilment of each one depend on the happiness, freedom and fulfilment of all. Moreover, if the group is to attain its goal, each individual has to maintain certain disciplines and make certain sacrifices for the sake of the group. Imagine that you're one of a party of mountaineers climbing Everest. You're obviously excited by the thought of achieving that goal and you want to do it. You've trained and got yourself in shape for the climb, as have your nine fellow climbers. If any of you is going to make it to the summit, you all need to consent to some basic rules before you start out. You agree not to wander off on your own, to carry your share of the common kit, to leave the final decision about your route to your leader. You accept that you must limit how much you eat so that there is enough for all, that you will share your gear if someone else loses theirs, that you will not abandon a colleague on the mountain. These are the sort of compacts mountaineers tend to make. They constitute a code of ethics, a set of shared values, that are crucial to any climb. Without them, everyone knows, mountains can be extremely dangerous: people can get injured, lost or frozen to death.

Such agreements are like ropes that hold the team together on the difficult ascent. When they are broken, tragedies happen. One of the horrors of the ascent to Everest is that the route to the summit takes you past the frozen bodies of those who have died in the attempt. Often, the reason they perished was that they were passed by other mountaineers who, with the summit in sight and at the limits of their own endurance, chose not to stop to help them but pressed on to their personal goal. The upper slopes of Everest are a chilling witness to that tendency in us that, in extreme circumstances, will put our own interests above the wellbeing of others, even if it means leaving them to die.

Could the same be said for some of the ruthless self-interest of businesses, governments and other organizations over the past two decades in particular? In the race for the summit and the rewards it offers, have we become horribly selfish, willing to close our eyes to the consequences for others around us? Have we, like those climbers, contravened the unwritten codes of behaviour that are so important if mountaineering is not to descend into moral chaos? The reality is that unrestrained growth—in the market, in a church, in our personal liberties—is dangerously unstable and risks catastrophe. Like mountaineers, we need an ethical framework, a shared set of values, if we are to make the ascent without sacrificing our humanity.

Reaction to the action

To see how this need is manifested in the ecology of power, we must look at what is diametrically opposite to the Affiliative strategy. If we look at our model, we see that opposite to PWX is R (reserved, or backstage), S (strong) and C (consolidating)—in other words, that what is required to balance the Affiliative strategy is the Foundational strategy. This RSC strategy needs to be in operation on the back stage if the frontstage PWX strategy is to be applied safely and responsibly. The RSC strategy is the one exemplified by Abraham Lincoln, in his appeals to the foundations of the Union as the moral and social basis for government. We saw that it is the agreed rules and boundaries, assumptions and expectations that sustain any social edifice, be it a family, school, church, business, state or nation.

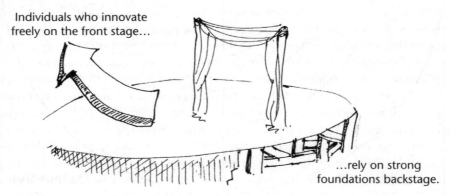

Individuals who innovate freely on the front stage...

...rely on strong foundations backstage.

If we are to enjoy the freedom of Affiliative leadership, it must stand on RSC foundations. It is interesting to note what Ronald Reagan had on his back stage. He was a committed Christian, whose morality was informed by the ethics and values he found in the Bible. He was not afraid to speak out on such issues as prayer in schools and abortion, though his aides warned him it hurt him in the polls. Abortion is wrong, he said, because it both kills and coarsens. There was a toughness to Reagan that many who knew him experienced as a kind of detachment: a willingness to set aside other people's feelings, as well as his own, for the sake of the cause he believed in. He always thought that it was his social and political message, rather than his manner, that had made a lasting impact. In his farewell address, he said: 'I never thought it was my style or the words I used that made a difference: it was the content. I wasn't a great communicator, but I communicated great things...' Underneath this lay a sense

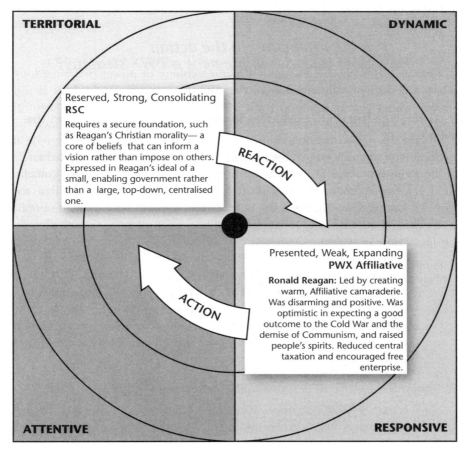

TERRITORIAL   **DYNAMIC**

Reserved, Strong, Consolidating
RSC

Requires a secure foundation, such as Reagan's Christian morality— a core of beliefs that can inform a vision rather than impose on others. Expressed in Reagan's ideal of a small, enabling government rather than a large, top-down, centralised one.

REACTION

Presented, Weak, Expanding
PWX Affiliative

Ronald Reagan: Led by creating warm, Affiliative camaraderie. Was disarming and positive. Was optimistic in expecting a good outcome to the Cold War and the demise of Communism, and raised people's spirits. Reduced central taxation and encouraged free enterprise.

ACTION

ATTENTIVE   **RESPONSIVE**

Diagram 8.1: Affiliative (PWX) action and RSC reaction

of an obligation to serve others that fed a desire to see people free. Reagan once said: 'The lessons of leadership were ... hard work, a knowledge of the facts, a willingness to listen and be understanding, a strong sense of duty and direction, and a determination to do your best on behalf of the people you serve.'

Without such a moral underpinning, PWX leadership descends into mere rampant aspirationalism, the kind of chaotic, ill-disciplined and unattractive indulgence you see in some families in which the children have not been given any boundaries to their self-expression and gratification. PWX leadership can function in a healthy way only if social and moral foundations have first been laid that define the shape of the edifice to be built on top of them. Perhaps it was this familial feeling of security that led one member of staff at the White House, parodying a 1950s TV show, to call out whenever Reagan came back, 'Daddy's home!' 'Daddy's home. A wise and brave and responsible man is running things. And that's a good way to feel,' Peggy Noonan recalled of Reagan in *Time* on 13 April 1998.

How does a leader implement a PWX strategy?

There are four key elements to implementing this strategy effectively:

1. Encourage the sharing of ideas for tackling issues that concern the whole team

- Invite suggestions for solving team-management issues. Asking others to help to find a solution requires them to try to understand the problem, to see it from other people's perspectives and to acknowledge the consequences of not solving it, and inevitably will remind them of their shared responsibility for causing it!
- Create your own, unique team 'contract' or 'agreement' which has been generated by all (for example, 'As a team, we agree always to take responsibility for our behaviour, always to listen in meetings...'). Once it is written up, get each member of the team to sign the sheet, including yourself, and display it for all to see. This is a wonderful way to make individuals accountable for their behaviour: it enables you to remind the team of the agreed rules and gives you criteria for what constitutes unacceptable behaviour.

2. Engender a sense of responsibility for learning

- Create a 'buddy' system in which everyone pairs with a colleague to help to solve each other's problems.

- Encourage people to try to solve their own problems on their own before asking for help. You might introduce the mantra 'brain, buddy, boss' as a way to remind them.
- Encourage independence and responsibility by allocating office jobs— someone to buy the croissants, someone to buy the flowers, someone to update the 'challenge' charts, someone to check whether projects are at 'red', 'amber' or 'green'.

3. Foster a culture of affirmation in the team

- Set an example in giving praise. People will notice and will start to use the same vocabulary.
- Set up a 'Gotcha! pot', into which a bit of pasta (say) is put every time someone is 'caught' doing something good, kind or helpful. When the pot is full, the whole team gets a reward—something the team itself can agree on. Set aside a small budget for these rewards, which need not be expensive. The key thing is that anyone can award a Gotcha! when they spot someone else doing something great, and in this way you foster a culture in which everyone is rewarded for noticing and affirming good practice.
- Set aside time in team meetings for opportunities to hear about and see each other's work.

4. Invite members of the team to create shared rituals and routines

- Have a birthday book.
- Bring croissants into the office every Thursday morning at 9am.
- Bring bags of sweets (one particular type?) to team meetings. Everyone loves sweets, even when they are on a diet!

Some examples of PWX leadership in action

- A mentor encouraging a protégée to work her way through problems facing her
- A man expressing his support and admiration for his wife as she begins a new career
- A team coach finding positive things to say about each individual's performance
- A line manager thanking someone for his contribution to the team and citing three specific ways in which his input is valued
- A teacher inviting the class to clap a child who normally struggles with good behaviour when she achieves a modest goal

- A sports team putting their arms round each other in a 'huddle' before a match

When to use a PWX strategy

- As the underlying approach in leadership, it ensures that the best is encouraged and released in people
- To create a culture of affirmation and praise when the mood has been critical or downbeat
- To foster an enabling leadership in which people are trusted to take responsibility
- To engender teamwork and mutual responsibility, breaking down barriers between groups or individuals
- With individuals whose confidence is low
- When a team has previously experienced a dominating, authoritarian, PSC leader and people therefore lack confidence in themselves
- Where a large element of team output is demanded, requiring individuals to work together

NINE

Jimmy Carter and the Serving Strategy
(RWX)

The political landscape on which Ronald Reagan strode with such confidence in 1981 had been a more uncertain place in 1976, when Jimmy Carter defeated the incumbent Gerald Ford in the presidential election. The Democrat candidate had been a dark horse and historians say that one of the principal reasons he won was the pardon Ford had granted to Richard Nixon after the Watergate scandal. It was often alleged (though never proved) that Ford and Nixon had made a pact that if the former succeeded to the presidency once Nixon had resigned, he would pardon his old boss. It was against this backdrop of moral uncertainty that Carter arrived in the White House: an earnest, well-meaning and deeply committed Christian man.

One of his first acts in office was to order the unilateral removal of all nuclear weapons from South Korea. He also announced his intention to remove all American troops from that country. In his first month as president, he cut the defence budget by $6 billion. His early instinct was to scale down America's military operations worldwide. The Vietnam War had ended the year before he took office, and Carter seemed uncomfortable with the high-profile, dominating approach of his predecessors. One of his most controversial achievements was the final negotiation of the Panama Canal Treaties, which were signed in September 1977. These in effect transferred control of the (American-built) canal to the state of Panama, and they were bitterly opposed by both the Republican Party and a section of the American public. The move was regarded as a major mistake, which reduced America's ability both to control the flow of goods through the canal and to extract revenue from it; yet it expressed Carter's moral instinct that power, control and ownership should be given, as far as possible, to local peoples rather than being retained in the hands of a centralized empire. His domestic policies similarly showed a commitment to decentralize services. He brought in strong environmental legislation, deregulated the trucking, airline, rail, finance, communications and oil industries and bolstered the social-security system. At the same time, reflecting his bias towards people who had been marginalized and overlooked, he appointed record numbers of women and people from ethnic minorities to significant positions in the government.

Carter's early posture in both domestic and foreign policy represented a marked shift from previous administrations. Small in stature and a man of strong religious convictions, he lacked the personal charisma and flair to dominate the public stage and seemed more at home in the roles of pastor and preacher than as president of the most powerful country on earth. His emphasis on the rights of others was not what Americans had come to expect from their leaders. That is not to say that previous administrations had been casual about human rights, but that such concerns had probably been seen as secondary to American growth and dominance. For Carter, they came first. Other things—economic success, military power, global political control—he believed would follow if America got its priorities right.

One incident is more revealing than any other about the workings of his mind. In 1979, the energy market collapsed, sending oil prices spiralling. Carter was due to deliver his fifth major speech on energy; but he felt that the American people were no longer listening and so instead he went to Camp David and for 10 days met with governors, mayors, religious leaders, scientists, economists and ordinary citizens. Sitting on the floor, he took notes on their comments, and especially wanted to hear criticism. His pollster told him that the people simply faced a crisis of confidence after the assassination of John F Kennedy, the Vietnam War and Watergate. Carter went on national television and said: 'I want to talk to you right now about a fundamental threat to American democracy. ... The threat is nearly invisible in ordinary ways. It is a crisis of confidence. It is a crisis that strikes at the very heart and soul and spirit of our national will. We can see this crisis in the growing doubt about the meaning of our own lives and in the loss of a unity of purpose for our nation.'

Carter's instinct was to listen rather than to command. He felt the need both to understand and to share in the problems of the people he led. Following the recommendations of the Department of Energy he had created, he wore sweaters, installed solar panels on the roof of the White House, installed a wood stove in his living quarters and ordered the General Services Administration to turn off the hot water supply in some government buildings. Across the country, thermostats were installed in both government and commercial buildings to stop people turning up the heating in the winter and the air conditioning in the summer.

There is something powerful and challenging about Carter's integrity in these choices. He felt deeply uncomfortable about calling on others to make sacrifices that he and his staff were not ready to make. The congruence of his words and actions was remarkable in a world in which so many politicians are busy constructing an image. He was willing to be openly vulnerable and ask for help: to reveal to the world his weakness rather than bluster and pretend to be strong. It is difficult to dismiss his conduct as anything other than authentic.

Authenticity is something that is mentioned a great deal in leadership thinking today. However, the reality is often rather less challenging and disconcerting than it should be. The leader who allows herself to identify personally with suffering is a rare creature. Of course, politicians put in brief appearances in slums and ghettos, but how many actually make sacrifices themselves that match those of the general population? As the people of Paris starved in 1789, Marie Antoinette was accused (wrongly, as it happens) of uttering the infamous words 'Let them eat cake!' George W Bush was severely criticized for his 'fly over' New Orleans after the devastation of Hurricane Katrina, rather than getting his feet (let alone his hands) dirty. We are quick to charge our leaders with hypocrisy, with saying one thing and doing another—and yet we are taken aback when we encounter a leader who is committed enough to get personally involved, in a costly, self-sacrificial way, in the cause they are working for.

In recent years, such a figure has been the Burmese democrat Aung San Suu Kyi. Held under house arrest in Rangoon for many years, she was given the opportunity by the military junta to travel to London, where her British husband (whom she had not seen for over three years) was dying of cancer. However, she suspected that once she had left the country she would not be allowed to return, and so she gave up the last chance to see her husband and chose instead to remain in Burma, in captivity alongside her people. On a smaller scale, in 2006, John Sentamu, the Archbishop of York (the second most important see in the Church of England), felt compelled to identify himself with the plight of the victims of war in the Middle East. Instead of waging a political campaign, however, he had his head shaved and spent a week living in the cathedral in a tent, praying and fasting. The sight of a purple-robed archbishop on his knees under canvas was both disturbing and compelling and there are several stories of people finding faith or hope after meeting him.

What the Serving strategy can achieve

This is the RWX Serving strategy. It involves the leader paying attention to the back stage of each situation rather than the front. Instead of concentrating on appearances and public perceptions and the management of political or corporate image, he chooses to attend to what is going on round the back, behind the scenes rather than in the limelight. Thus, Carter sensed that behind the scenes the American people were no longer listening, they were gripped by some unease, some angst, and he needed to listen to this and understand it before he acted. And on this back stage the leader *keeps his emotional and strategic boundaries open* (using weak rather than strong force). Instead of having a set policy or approach that he is going to follow no matter what, he seeks to respond to the needs of each situation even as they emerge. He chooses to allow himself to submit to the agenda of those around him and follow that— rather like a good sister in charge of a hospital ward, who knows the needs of her patients and is always busy moving from one situation to another.

One of the most potent counters to the emphasis on the competence, strength and dominance of leaders over the past two decades has been Robert K Greenleaf's book *Servant Leadership*. His original essay 'The Servant as Leader' set out what he saw as the antithesis between 'the servant-led leader' and 'the leader-led servant'. 'The servant-leader is servant first. ... He or she is sharply different from the person who is leader first, perhaps because of the need to assuage an unusual power drive or to acquire material possessions. For such it will be a later choice to serve—after leadership is established.' For Greenleaf, there is a clear moral difference between leading others from a desire to dominate and leading them from a desire to serve. This perspective has rightly found a powerful voice in a leadership industry that all too often cultivates (whether overtly or covertly) the power of the leader to dominate.

Many have seen echoes of religion in the paradigm of the servant-leader. For many in the Christian church, the phrase is deeply evocative of the language

Jesus used about himself and about the call to leadership. One day, two of his disciples were squabbling about which of them was the more important. When Jesus heard them, he said: 'If anyone wants to be first, he must be the very last, and the servant of all' (Mark 9.35). He went on to say that this priority was crucial to his own identity, for 'the Son of Man did not come to be served, but to serve, and to give his life as a ransom for many' (Mark 10.45). Jesus epitomized this in the way he spent time with the rejects of his day, the homeless, the sick, the dysfunctional, the overlooked. He hung out with those who were weak and poor—indeed, it was usually the rich and the powerful who opposed him, in part because they were shamed by his generosity. Jesus saw beauty in those whom others thought ugly, and potential in those whom others had written off. His paradoxical 'last shall be first' teachings were nowhere more explicit than in what has come to be known as the Beatitudes: the list of blessings he promises for those who seek the kingdom of God. 'Blessed are the poor in spirit, for theirs is the kingdom of heaven. Blessed are those who mourn, for they will be comforted. Blessed are the meek, for they will inherit the earth...' (Matthew 5.3-5).

Two years later, when Jesus got down on his knees to wash the calloused feet of his disciples, an act that only a servant would be expected to do, it was so unsettling that one of them, Simon Peter, at first refused to let him to do it. He couldn't reconcile the lordship of Jesus with such a menial task. His own paradigm of power and leadership resisted the idea that his Lord should do anything so humiliating. Jesus' life of service was problematic also for the leaders of his day, as it has been for others since. The Jews were waiting for a Messiah who would overthrow the imperial rule of Rome. Muslims believe that Jesus was rescued from the cross before he died, as it is impossible that a great prophet could die in such a way. The servanthood of Jesus, which is at the centre of the Christian faith, is deeply disconcerting.

In recent decades, figures such as Mahatma Gandhi, Mother Teresa and Archbishop Desmond Tutu have likewise been deeply unsettling in the way they have poured out their lives sacrificially for the good of others, pricking our consciences and compelling us to reconsider our attitude to others. However, as *leaders* they are all too easily dismissed as mavericks and eccentrics. Of course, it is true that there is a difference between a politician and a prophet, a statesman and a servant—these callings are not the same. But does that have to mean that a politician cannot be a prophet as well, and a statesman can't be a servant? It all depends on how that service is practised.

Arguably, the failure of someone like Carter to succeed as a political leader was due not to his attitude of service (which only gave him authenticity) but to his inability to act decisively and with appropriate strength when required. Two days after his speech about America's 'malaise', and in the face of the energy crisis, Carter asked for the resignations of his entire Cabinet. In his eyes, this was a necessary admission that so far his administration had failed. However, to the public it gave the impression that the White House was in disarray. It undermined people's confidence in the president and his administration at a time when what they needed was reassurance. It left people feeling lost and adrift.

Again, it demonstrated perfectly the impact of the RWX strategy of leadership. Instead of taking a strong lead on the front stage, Carter admitted that he, too, was struggling to cope with the situation. He was listening, but he was not pretending that he had all the solutions. The Serving strategy always pushes responsibility firmly back onto the followers. In a sense, the leader refuses to solve the problem for them, rejects their calls to fix it, to make it all better. Instead, he encourages them to attend to the problem, as he is doing, so that they can find the solution together. It is undoubtedly a more honest strategy, and one that in the long run fosters greater maturity, responsibility and understanding in followers; but at the time it is unsettling. It's essential that followers should feel a deep trust that the leader is still big enough not to be overwhelmed by events.

In the end, this was Carter's fatal weakness: he could not show that he was big enough not to be overwhelmed by events. Chief among these, perhaps, was the hostage crisis. On 4 November 1979, the American embassy in Tehran was seized by Iranian students. The overthrow of the Shah by Islamist revolutionaries earlier in the year had led to a steady deterioration in relations between Iran and America, and when the exiled Shah was allowed to go to America for medical treatment, a crowd of about five hundred seized the embassy and the ninety-odd people inside it. Carter applied economic pressure by freezing Iranian assets in America and halting imports of Iranian oil, and at the same time began several diplomatic initiatives to secure the release of the hostages. When all of these measures proved fruitless, on 24 April 1980 the armed forces attempted a rescue mission. That, too, failed. After three out of eight helicopters were disabled or crashed in the Iranian desert, the operation was aborted, with eight American personnel dead. In the end, after 440 days in captivity, the last 52 hostages were released on the day Carter left office. The crisis had been a devastating blow to national prestige.

This apparent weakness in Carter's approach seems to have been one of the factors that prompted a dramatic change of tack in his foreign policy. After the Soviets invaded Afghanistan in 1979, Carter announced what became known as the Carter Doctrine: that America would not allow any outside power to gain control of the Persian Gulf. He terminated the wheat deal that Nixon had made with the Soviet Union to promote détente and prohibited Americans from participating in the 1980 summer Olympics in Moscow. He reinstated registration for the draft for young men, to rebuild America's military power. He also commenced a covert $40-billion programme to train Islamic mujahidin in Pakistan and Afghanistan. Ronald Reagan would later expand this programme greatly as a way to contain the Soviet Union. Today, critics blame both presidents for the resulting instability in post-Soviet Afghanistan, which led to the rise of Islamic theocracy in the region and also created much of the current problem of Islamic fundamentalism.

Reaction to the action

This unexpected switch from Carter's instinctive Serving posture to one of greater aggression and domination illustrates the strange paradox that lies at the heart of the RWX strategy. In the ecology of power, this is paired with the Commanding PSC strategy. The act of serving, if you like, vacates space for others to impose their own control. It allows others to come onto the front stage and dictate events, as both the Iranian students and the Soviets did. At the same time, if the Serving leader feels that things are slipping away from him, he may suddenly conclude that he needs to reassert control on the front stage and often his response is a PSC one. It is rather like the panicky reaction of the driver who, having allowed his child to hold the steering wheel for a while, suddenly finds himself wrenching it back again as the car heads towards a tree; or the teacher who, having given her students a free rein in the classroom, suddenly senses that they are taking advantage and things have gone too far, and she then clamps down much more severely than she normally does.

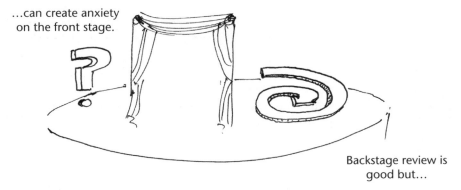

...can create anxiety on the front stage.

Backstage review is good but...

This kind of action and reaction is characteristic of the RWX approach. It explains why Carter's contribution to the political scene after his presidency has met with a mixed reaction. He has campaigned for human rights and other causes, striven to resolve conflict and eradicate disease, and in particular worked tirelessly with Habitat for Humanity, which builds affordable homes in partnership with poor families. Nonetheless, his interventions are seen by some as unhelpful. They object to his criticisms of subsequent administrations and what he sees as their unjust policies, and protest at his readiness to listen to and mediate on behalf of what others regard as brutal regimes. Carter is still a powerful figure, but his power lies as much in what he *failed* to deliver as in what he succeeded in doing. For some, he recalls the confusion and indignity of a president of the United States of America sitting on the floor listening to religious leaders and environmentalists, installing wood-burning stoves in the White House, proving impotent to free hostages. His image, like any other Serving leader, destabilizes our perceptions of power and challenges us to look again at what we really want from our leaders. We play lip-service to the ideals of integrity and authenticity, but in reality we want leaders who are strong. We deride the greed of some business executives but at the same time find

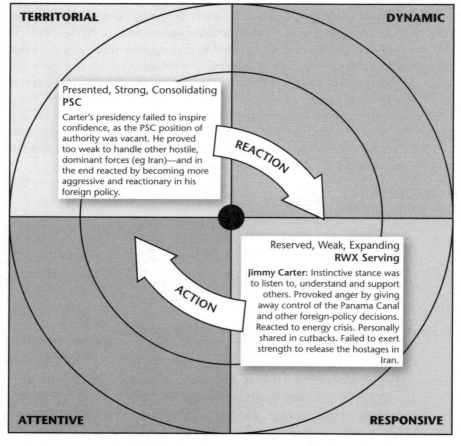

Diagram 9.1: Serving (RWX) action and PSC reaction

it unsettling if a CEO lives modestly and drives a Ford. There is a disturbing inconsistency in our own attitude to power when we encounter a leader who serves us. And perhaps that is why the RWX strategy is one of the most potent of all for a leader to employ.

How does a leader implement an RWX strategy?

There are four key elements to implementing this strategy effectively:

1. Identify with the situation of those you lead

- The Serving leader accepts that, first and foremost, she must identify with her followers. Instead of remaining detached, she opts to be involved.
- She may do this by physically being with her followers—working on the shop floor, helping out in the kitchen, doing menial jobs, listening to what people want to say to her. (Sir Terry Leahy, CEO of Tesco—the biggest retailer in Britain, which in 2005 made a profit of £2.2 billion—is renowned for spending time at the checkout, in jeans and open-necked shirt, listening to his shop assistants.
- The Serving leader shares the privations of her followers as well as their triumphs.

2. Allow individuals a chance to develop their own solutions

- Don't be afraid of silence. Giving people time and space is imperative if they are to learn to navigate their problems.
- Unresolved problems should be acknowledged and given attention, but not necessarily solved immediately. RWX needs to become RSX before you will generate good solutions.
- In meetings, it's very important that you convey to people by both your words and your expressions that you are being patient and supportive. Be comfortable being silent!
- Aim to resource ideas and initiatives from the background, so that others will enjoy their success.

3. Resist intervening too soon to resolve social tensions

- Give people time and space to deal with their mutual disagreements and frustrations. Waiting just a little while can encourage people to work things out and find their own solutions. Obviously, if a situation appears to be escalating it's important that you should apply a different strategy (for example PSC, if you need to take control in an authoritative way). 'Putting your foot down' straightaway can limit other people's opportunities to try out social skills, such as listening to other points of view, or to see the effect of their unkind words on other people.

· By observing social tensions, you can learn important things about people and the way they relate to others, and on reflection you can see how they are developing socially, and what sort of experiences and personalities challenge them. You will also find it very effective to have specific illustrations to share with the team when it comes to feedback.

4. Negotiate the mess

· Rather than denying and suppressing a messy situation, or trying to fix it while remaining detached, get involved.

· Others may be paralysed by the situation, but you should show confidence that a brighter future is attainable and should offer hope.

Some examples of RWX leadership in action

· An executive taking time to go round the office, listening to his staff or making cups of coffee

· A surgeon visiting her patient late at night after an operation, just to make sure they are settled before she leaves the hospital

· A host clearing up in the kitchen while the guests at his dinner party enjoy coffee

· A golf caddy supporting his player, carrying his bags, measuring distances and so on

· A teacher moving round the class, helping individual children who are stuck on an exercise

· A consultant brought in to address an IT problem, working invisibly in the background to fix it

· A government making a pact with a potential enemy to deal with something inimical to both

· A nurse caring for the patients on his ward

· Two parties reaching a covert deal before formal negotiations begin

· An executive taking a pay cut in lean times, to show solidarity with her workers

When to use an RWX strategy

· When your followers face a steep challenge, for which you must release them but also prepare them

- When you are using the Commanding PSC strategy in a situation. This should be counterpointed consciously and intentionally with a policy of serving, in little ways, to win respect and trust.
- When people are fragile or hurting, as an act of service
- To model authenticity in your own life by matching your words and your actions
- To encourage others to take responsibility and trust themselves rather than depending on you

TEN

Winston Churchill and the Pacesetting Strategy (PSX)

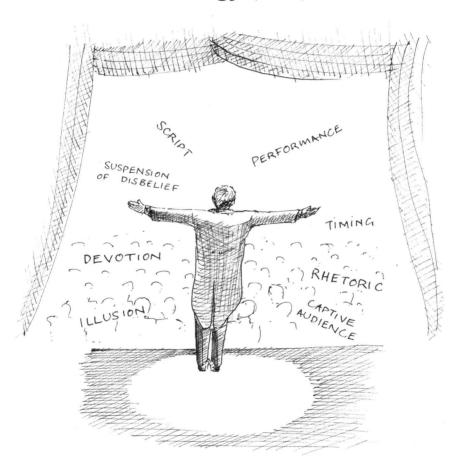

Sir Winston Leonard Spencer Churchill was a man who believed that his destiny was to bestride human history. In total contrast to the humility of Carter, or the modesty of Lincoln, or even the humorous warmth of Reagan, his ego was magnificently dominant. F S Oliver, the Conservative pamphleteer and historian, offered the following appraisal of his personality: 'From his youth up Mr. Churchill has loved with all his heart, with all his mind, with all his soul, and with all his strength, three things: war, politics and himself. He has loved war for its dangers, he loves politics for the same reason, and himself he has always loved for the knowledge that his mind is dangerous—dangerous to his enemies, dangerous to his friends, dangerous to himself. I can think of no man I have ever met who would so quickly and so bitterly eat his heart out in Paradise.'

He was a man of enormous ambition and energy, and yet for a long time the trajectory of his political career was as wide of its target as a misfired shell from one of the great warships he so loved. It was not until 1940, after the outbreak of the Second World War, at the age of 65, with the best part of 40 years in political life behind him, that Churchill was able finally to find his range. (Or perhaps it was that the target itself had moved to where he was aiming.) From that point onward, however, his contribution was immense and extraordinary. Churchill was to leave a legacy unsurpassed in modern prime-ministerial history in Britain—so much so that in 2002 (forgetting perhaps that he was half-American), the public voted him the greatest Briton ever.

Far and away the larger part of his political career had been erratic and often undistinguished. He suffered notable failures throughout his career, not least in the debacle at Gallipoli in 1915–16. Churchill proposed a plan to bring the First World War to an end by opening up a new front in Turkey. Through what appears to have been a combination of miscommunication and misfortune, the campaign became a disaster. In the first, naval attack, Britain had six out of nine battleships put out of action, three of them sunk. The subsequent amphibious assault was followed by nine months of fruitless fighting in which the Allies lost 46,000 dead before they were forced to withdraw, defeated. Churchill carried much of the blame and by the end of the year had resigned from the government.

Throughout his career, his big asset (but also his biggest problem) was that he saw everything in terms of the great global drama of political and military history. After the end of the First World War, his chief anxiety was the rearmament of Germany. Having struggled (and himself experienced battle) against an enemy that had, as he put it, 'almost single-handedly fought nearly all the world and nearly beat them,' Churchill issued what proved to be prophetic warnings during the emergence of Nazism and Adolf Hitler's rise to power throughout the 1920s and '30s. At the time, there was no appetite for such talk. The climate was one of appeasement. The cost of the last war, in both lives and money, was still being counted. Few people had either the emotional or the financial resources to face the threat of another confrontation with a resurgent, belligerent Germany. Churchill, however, always had the stomach for a fight. The image of him as the British bulldog standing up to Hitler that lives in the memory of anyone who witnessed the Blitz or other crucial battles of 1940, epitomizes the pugnacious spirit of this indomitable man.

Domestic politics is, on the whole, not as dramatic as war, nor does it usually call for great heroes. On its more mundane and pragmatic stage, Churchill's larger-than-life performance diminished between the two world wars and he was reduced to minor roles in which he could be more easily managed. He had always used the media to the hilt and he got his message about the state of Europe across through a series of commissioned articles in the *Evening Standard*. He cultivated relationships with newspaper proprietors such as Lord Beaverbrook, and when his opinions differed from theirs he would find other channels through which to express them. In 1938, when his contract with the *Standard* was terminated after a disagreement with Beaverbrook, he managed to get his articles read by millions through the *News of the World*, which was syndicated throughout both Europe and the Empire. At the same time, he churned out book after book about great British figures (including his own ancestors) and famous military campaigns. His approach to history was to write it himself; his approach to his own place in history was the same. Churchill understood the need to manage the story that was told both about world affairs and about his role in them. His instinct was always to intervene and to influence. To leave history to be written by other individuals, or even to emerge by consensus, was alien to his sense of purpose.

His unique character and role illustrate *in extremis* the leader who pursues the PSX Pacesetting strategy. We might note that he was always more at home on the front stage of politics—and the front benches of the House of Commons—than the back. 'No informed person could well deny that Winston S Churchill was probably the most spectacular showman in the history of British politics,' wrote the influential American scholar Harry Elmer Barnes.[7] Certainly, he cultivated an image quite deliberately. The cigar-chewing, victory-sign-waving, growling persona was one he adopted extensively throughout the war—he was aware that he needed to 'put it on' before going out to meet the public. He also cultivated his reputation for sharp one-liners, rehearsing quips and repartees to give him the edge in debate.

He appreciated the need to manage the front stage when communicating with the public, especially in times of high emotion or anxiety. On 4 August 1912, nine Boy Scouts, all from working-class communities in south-east London, were drowned when their boat capsized on a sailing trip down the Thames to the Isle of Sheppey. In a grand gesture, Churchill, then First Lord of

---

[7] From *The Journal of Historical Review*, Summer 1980 (Vol 1, No 1), pp163–68

the Admiralty, immediately ordered that their bodies should be brought back up the river on board a destroyer. As *HMS Fervent* sailed slowly up the Thames, thousands of people gathered on the banks to mourn the loss of innocent life. Churchill understood that working men and women would be touched and comforted more by such a gesture of respect than by any formal act of remembrance.

Perhaps his most famous frontstage acts of communication were in his speeches and his radio broadcasts to the nation in 1940, as the threat of invasion loomed. 'I have nothing to offer but blood, toil, tears and sweat,' he told the House of Commons in his first appearance as Prime Minister. He followed that closely with three more, equally famous declarations. After the defeat at Dunkirk, he assured an anxious nation: 'We shall defend our island, whatever the cost may be. We shall fight on the beaches, we shall fight on the landing grounds, we shall fight in the fields and in the streets, we shall fight in the hills; we shall never surrender.' As the Battle of Britain loomed, he urged: 'Let us therefore brace ourselves to our duties, and so bear ourselves that, if the British Empire and its Commonwealth last for a thousand years, men will still say, "This was their finest hour."' And at the height of the Battle, his bracing survey of the situation included the memorable line: 'Never in the field of human conflict was so much owed by so many to so few.'

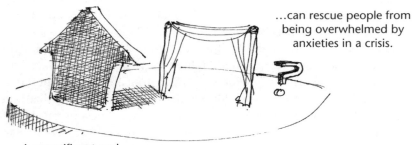

...can rescue people from being overwhelmed by anxieties in a crisis.

A magnificent and compelling frontstage presence...

Above all, Churchill had a sense of timing. When he was finally appointed Prime Minister, he recorded that 'all my past life had been but a preparation for this hour and for this trial.' He also understood what people needed to hear and feel, and when. He was at home with the hyperbole of the moment: when the front stage was his and his alone, and the audience was gripped with fear before some mighty threat, he was at his best. In such circumstances, he seemed to grow in stature, rising to the epic occasion. Rather than being crushed by the odds stacked against him, he relished the confrontation. He used strong, rather than weak, power almost exclusively, demanding loyalty, commitment, energy, will and self-belief from those who (very much) followed in his wake. Collaboration, discussion and consensual decision-making were foreign concepts to him. So was moderation. He was notorious for his interference in the details of military operations, finding it hard to cede authority and autonomy to those under him. His 'Action this day!' memos were like a stream of consciousness he wanted implemented without debate throughout the war. He wrote in excess, drank in excess and commanded in excess. Those who served under him at that time could scarcely keep up with him, often despite being many years his junior. His instinct was always to take the battle to the enemy; retreat was rarely an option. Expanding rather than consolidating was his strategy.

These are the hallmarks of the Pacesetting leader, frontstage, strong and expanding: relentless confidence, apparently limitless drive, indomitable will, commanding presence, compelling personality, dominating authority, with vast horizons in a heroic enterprise. In the end, PSX leadership is all about the leader himself; it is his own ego projected onto a social or historical canvas, compelling circumstances around him to conform to his personal will.

What the Pacesetting strategy can achieve

There are, of course, only certain contexts in which such leadership is desirable or even tolerable. In the main, it is needed in a situation where winning is the only acceptable goal. It was necessary for Churchill, confronting the threat of a Nazi victory in Europe. It is necessary also in competitive sport. In both situations, the conflict or confrontation is specific and relatively limited in duration. Events conspire to create a particular window in which victory must be achieved; in this window, one's entire effort, and that of the team, organization, army or country one is leading, must be focused on that goal. You exert every fibre in your body, draw on all your reserves, to resist your enemy's attacks and to win. PSX leadership demands in the leader an unfailing confidence of victory even in the face of defeat.

In 2003, Martin Johnson led England to a famous victory in the Rugby Union World Cup in Sydney. The win was attributed largely to the inspirational leadership of Clive Woodward, the head coach, who had managed the preparations for this tournament over the previous seven years. The character of Woodward's leadership was essentially PSX. He had always said (and believed) that his team would win the World Cup; he never looked back and always moved quickly on from any defeat. He spared no expense on the latest and best training methods, and fostered a culture in which only winning mattered, ruthlessly ditching players who were out of form regardless of their reputation. Some commentators argue that the World Cup was won before a single game had been played: other teams simply wilted before England's ruthless imposition of its will.

Of course, there is nothing moral or good in itself about such dominance. The 'will to power' is entirely Nietzschean, and we know that it can be used as easily to abuse as to liberate. You could argue that Churchill's opponent Hitler was a similarly gifted and driven PSX leader. In fact, as many commentators have pointed out, he was in many ways the more disciplined and focused man, whose ideology opposed drunkenness, laziness and immorality and advocated self-sacrifice in the cause. Like Churchill, however, Hitler used the emotional dynamics of PSX power—in his massed rallies, his epic depictions of the struggles of the Reich after the First World War and the sense he conveyed of the place in history of the Aryan race. The danger of PSX leadership is that it demands of its followers utter loyalty and submission to the cause, whether it is good or bad.

Even when the cause is good, PSX leadership can sometimes leave a mixed legacy. I used to be involved in an organization that ran houseparties to introduce schoolchildren to the Christian faith. Its strategy, devised by its founder in the 1930s, was to concentrate on the top 30 private schools in the country—Eton, Harrow and so on—to target the people who would one day play a strategic part in the leadership of the country. The houseparties were of extraordinary benefit to me and many thousands of others who were nurtured in their faith in adolescence and on into early adulthood. The organization showed many of the classic signs of PSX leadership: it was well run and effective, with a strategic goal, a charismatic and compelling leader, a heroic sense of mission, a belief in its own historic importance and a demand for total loyalty from its staff and volunteers. I recall giving up an opportunity to tour Japan with my university track and field team in order to help out on a week-long revision houseparty for 16-year-olds.

One outcome of those houseparties was to school a generation of leaders who went on to wield influence at the highest level in the church, in education and even in politics. That organization was like an express train speeding towards its destination, and its progress was extraordinary. However, a lot of people have fallen off the train along the way. It doesn't stop for anyone—if you're on board, you're expected to stay on, adhering to everything required of you in belief and behaviour. If you can't keep up with the pace or live up to expectations, you simply go out the window. PSX organizations almost always leave a wake of broken, disillusioned people behind them. Of course, those still involved in them scarcely notice: they have already moved on, too focused on the goal to worry about those who couldn't make it.

The reaction to the action

Personally, I will always be grateful for the impact of those summer houseparties; but I am grateful for the experience of some of the pitfalls of PSX leadership as well as its benefits. It can cause problems not only for the organization but also for the leader herself. Its intensity is rarely sustainable for long. Typically, a PSX leader suffers periods of burnout and collapse. Churchill's life was blighted by a periodic depression, which became so familiar to him he dubbed it his 'black dog'. What such leaders have to fear is that when the spotlight is not on them, they often find it hard to know who they are. Their sense of self is so bound up with their public image and the power associated with it that outside that context anxiety and self-doubt can creep in. Coupled with their exhaustion after their tremendous exertion on the front stage, this means that such a leader

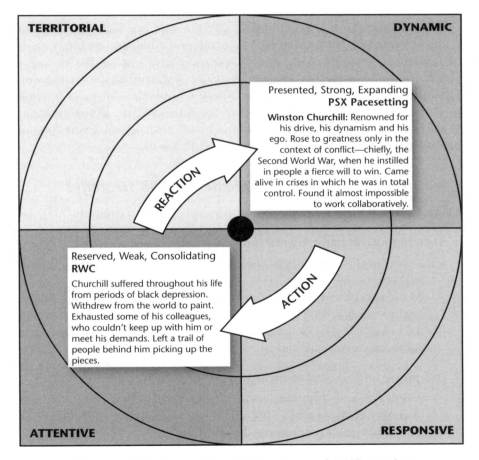

Diagram 10.1: Pacesetting (PSX) action and RWC reaction

may be vulnerable and unstable and may finally withdraw. The reaction PSX generates in the ecology of power is RWC—reserved, empty and passive, the squeezed-out lemon after the juice has flavoured the meal.

PSX leadership is leadership for a season, for a very particular kind of context, where the heightened drama of a confrontation or competition makes the most extreme demands. Leaders who choose to use this strategy need to recognize this—and also need to be aware that the followers of a PSX leader may reject him when the crisis has passed. Churchill experienced just such a desertion in 1945 even before the war was finally over, when, after he had led the country through its 'darkest hour' to victory in Europe, his party was voted out of government. In a similar way, Woodward's demands for even greater control following England's World Cup victory were resisted, and this ultimately led to his resignation. Followers can live with the intensity in times of crisis, but rarely want it in times of stability.

Nonetheless, the rare contribution a PSX leader can make at the right moment has resulted in some of the finest and most admirable demonstrations of leadership in history. This style of leadership also inspires the strongest attachment in followers. On 3 September 1939, when Britain declared war on Germany and the then Prime Minister, Neville Chamberlain, invited Churchill to join his War Cabinet as First Lord of the Admiralty, the signal went out to every naval ship and base: 'Winston is back!' Such is the devotion—and dependence—that can be generated by a great PSX leader.

How does a leader implement a PSX strategy?

There are four key elements to implementing this strategy effectively:

1. Seek to motivate and inspire using yourself

- Believe in your authority to command and lead people—PSX is all about backing yourself!
- At the start of a new piece of work, consciously try to change pace. This might include talking in a more animated and 'projected' way, standing up taller, using your hands as you speak, choosing more dynamic vocabulary than usual and so on.

2. Use praise and reward as means to celebrate effort and success

- When someone has done something well, draw it to the attention of others enthusiastically. It's important to choose a wide variety of individuals who have performed to their limits.

3. Set goals for individuals and groups

- Use a simple 'Next big challenge' sheet to monitor the team's progress. A 'challenge' might be to deliver a report by a deadline, visit a certain percentage of stakeholders or reduce waste by so many per cent.
- Make sure the challenges change frequently. The sense of achievement and momentum is what you are after. Any challenge that lasts longer than four weeks is probably too long.
- Use red, amber and green 'lights' to indicate how confident and how effective the team is in each project. A green light means: 'We're all systems go.' An amber says: 'We're moving, but could go faster.' A red says: 'We're stuck and need help to get going again.'

4. Make your standards explicit and be available

- Show the team what a project should look like when it is finished to a high standard.
- Make it clear how people can come to you with issues and problems. PSX leadership always tends to produce withdrawn, RWC behaviour in some people.
- Spend time 'on the ground' being available. Don't be remote or even absent when you are pursuing a PSX strategy.

Some examples of PSX leadership in action

- A sales department planning how to increase market share through more aggressive marketing tactics
- A coach pushing an athlete with a strict, ambitious training regime before a major competition
- A charismatic leader persuading her community to follow her on a risky path they would otherwise have avoided
- A mother promising a trip to a theme park 'once the Star Chart has been completed'
- A confident and lively child in the playground inventing a new, imaginative game and persuading others to join in
- An executive demanding a 10-per-cent increase in performance from his sales staff in the second quarter

When to use a PSX strategy

· In a competitive situation, to drive up performance
· When faced with a threat that requires self-belief and aggressive determination
· To motivate people to give their best
· To set an example for others to follow
· For short periods of time to inject a sense of urgency and excitement
· To give people experience of winning and losing

ELEVEN

Martin Luther King and the Visionary Strategy (RSX)

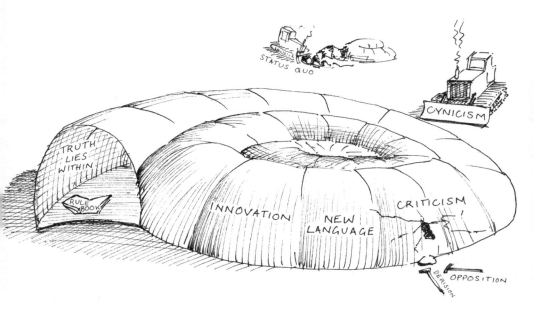

Among those images of the second half of the 20th century most deeply seared into the Western mind is one of an animated young black man with his arm raised, his finger pointing to the sky, as he addresses a huge rally. The man, of course, is Martin Luther King, and the date is 28 August 1963. He is delivering the speech that climaxes in one of the most widely known and quoted lines of modern times: 'I have a dream...'

King's was a life summed up by that one, single phrase. He was compelled by a dream of the end of the racial segregation that had endured in America, and in particular the southern states, since the civil war nearly a century earlier. King had experienced that segregation at first hand. He had been excluded from white educational institutions, been refused service at milk bars that were for whites only, been obliged to give up his seat on a bus for a white person; he had experienced imprisonment and would ultimately suffer assassination for the dream that one day such segregation would come to an end.

What set him apart from his fellow black Americans was three things: the advantage of education, a calling to religious leadership and a deep, burning passion against the injustices suffered by his community. Others had one or two of those attributes, but in King they converged into a vocation that drove him into the centre stage of one of the most momentous dramas in recent American history. He had take his doctorate at Boston University and was by nature a studious man. His knowledge of theology, biblical scholarship and political theory funded a career not in academia or the church but in political activism. His later speeches and, especially, his open letters to his fellow clergy reveal how in those earlier years of study he laid down an understanding of social justice and the rule of God that enabled him to think deeply about them. Like most activists—and all the more because he had a young family and because he was caught up in the stream of confrontations and crises that only grew stronger throughout the 1960s—he had comparatively little time for study and reflection later in his life. You get the sense that he drew heavily on the wells of thought he had bored as a young man. Whether or not they would ever have dried up we will never know, as his life was cut short at the age of only 39.

Second, King was informed by a sense that he was called to the ministry. Though he was to serve for only a short period as a pastor, in a local church in Montgomery, Alabama, his roots in the church and his fellowship with other Christians, both black and white, gave depth and breadth to his vision and filled it with confidence. At the heart of his thinking on desegregation lay a theological conviction, that all human beings are equal: equally created in the image of God, and so equally able to share in the benefits and rights of civil society. It was also his theology that prevented King from embracing the doctrine of black supremacy that some in the Black Power movement were promoting. For him, the Civil Rights movement was never about black domination but about black freedom.

Third, King was a man fuelled by righteous indignation at the injustices he witnessed around him. Perhaps because he himself had had a stable, loving home, he didn't have the slightly cowed mentality of some of his fellow blacks. He had seen how many simply accepted their place in society and made no protest at the way they were marginalized; but he was sufficiently sure of his own dignity not only to resist such treatment but also to believe that it could and should be resisted by others, too.

Most historians date the beginning of the modern civil rights movement in America as 1 December 1955. That was the day when, in Montgomery, an obscure 42-year-old seamstress called Rosa Parks refused to give up her seat on a bus to a white man. Her solitary act of defiance began a movement that was to end legal segregation in America. It so happened that King was the pastor of Dexter Avenue Baptist Church in Montgomery. He had arrived with his family just a few months earlier and was still finding his feet, but as the trial of Mrs Parks on 5 December approached, encouraged by others in the black community, he felt compelled to lead some kind of protest. What developed was the first of many boycotts of the buses in cities across the country. King soon became a mix of organizer and mouthpiece. He was involved in public meetings that rallied support, as it was vital, if the protest was to be effective, that the entire black community took part in it. Otherwise, if even a few had continued to use the buses, the symbolic significance of the boycott might have been lost. The protest depended on the power of collective action—not least in arranging other means of transport, for otherwise black workers who had ridden to work every day on the buses would risk losing their jobs. If you had been in Montgomery over Christmas and the New Year in 1955/6, you would have seen an unusual sight: many black people walking miles to work while others cycled or were ferried by those who owned cars and taxis. The boycott went on for over a year and the immense organization required put a strain on everyone involved, not least King.

The response of the white community was predictable enough. Imaginary traffic offences were invented and people were arrested. One night, returning home from a meeting by car and keeping well under the speed limit, King himself was stopped and taken in on a trumped-up charge. Only a few weeks later, things turned much nastier and, while King was out speaking at a meeting, his home and family were fire-bombed. Mercifully, neither Coretta, his wife, nor his children were injured. The opposition to the dream had started, and it was time to discover whether the vision had any substance.

The struggle that was to follow lasted 12 more years. The key strategies of the Civil Rights movement were devised and orchestrated by King and his close followers and included mass civil disobedience, or 'passive resistance'—the form of opposition first used by Gandhi and his followers in South Africa some 60 years earlier and then developed in the struggle for India's independence in the 1940s. Civil disobedience involved a peaceful refusal to comply with an unjust demand. So, when the authorities banned a protest march, the demonstrators would assemble and walk in peace nonetheless. When the police used batons and water cannons to disperse them, even though they were doing nothing to deserve arrest or provoke violence, their response was entirely peaceful. When they were beaten, they took the blows. When they were arrested, they did not resist. Indeed, part of the idea was simply to overwhelm the bureaucracies that imposed this injustice. The courts and the prisons couldn't cope with the numbers they had to deal with and at times they broke down. Meanwhile, the publicity the strategy was generating in the media was massive and, in general, highly favourable.

Increasingly, King's task was to be a figurehead, standing in front of his people and calling them on to the Promised Land of a desegregated America. It was in this role that he delivered some of his most memorable and visionary sermons and speeches. His rhetoric was highly visual and used concrete imagery to drive home the legitimacy of black people's claims. In 1968, he gave an address that included these words, which illustrate his straightforward use of extended metaphor. 'In a sense, we've come to our nation's capital to cash a cheque. When the architects of our republic wrote the magnificent words of the Constitution and the Declaration of Independence, they were signing a promissory note to which every American was to fall heir. This note was a promise that all men, yes, black men as well as white men, would be guaranteed the "inalienable rights" of "life, liberty and the pursuit of happiness". It is obvious today that America has defaulted on this promissory note, insofar as her citizens of colour are concerned. Instead of honouring this sacred obligation, America has given the Negro people a bad cheque, a cheque which has come back marked "insufficient funds". But we refuse to believe that the bank of justice is bankrupt. We refuse to believe that there are insufficient funds in the great vaults of opportunity of this nation. And so, we've come to cash this cheque, a cheque that will give us upon demand the riches of freedom and the security of justice.'

King drew on traditions of African-American folk preaching in which spiritual and invisible concerns are highly materialized as actual, felt realities. Critics have often pointed out that he was a plagiarist and that large sections of his addresses were taken from other people's sermons. I wouldn't want to condone that, but I think it is an indication that he chose to speak the language of the street, to use rhetoric that would connect with his followers. The real motive force behind his leadership, however, was his sense that he had glimpsed the future of which he spoke. In this respect, he was a seer: a prophet who not only pronounced judgement on the injustice of the structures around him but also foresaw that they could not stand in the face of legitimate protest.

I believe King's life exemplified the use of the RSX strategy and illustrated its power more vividly than anyone else in recent years. It may seem strange to locate his influence on the 'reserved' back stage rather than on the 'presented' front stage. Certainly, King made use of the front stage. Like Churchill, he became adept at public speaking, and his sense of timing and drama was important to the impact of the civil rights campaign. But, unlike Churchill, King didn't speak from a position of power on the front stage of government. Churchill was the central figure in the authority system of his day in Britain; King, however, was excluded from any such position of power. It is only in more recent times that his black successors such as Jesse Jackson, Colin Powell and Condoleezza Rice have found it possible to gain acceptance in the halls of power in Washington. In King's day, he could only protest. However influential, his was a voice from the political margins. In a sense, he lived on and spoke from the hidden-away back stage of American society—the part that many people wanted to be suppressed. He spoke for, and to, the conscience of America about the consequences of its frontstage politics and economics. In this regard, he didn't have at his disposal any of the kinds of power at his disposal his opponents had. He didn't have the authority to impeach politicians or prosecute police officers who attacked peaceful demonstrators. He didn't have the influence to get state legislation on desegregation changed. In this regard, his power lay in more subversive strategies that undermined the moral legitimacy of the regime that he and his followers opposed.

Nor, however, did he accept the status quo and simply empathize with the suffering of his people. Like Churchill, he compelled the black population—some of whom were reluctant to follow his lead—to find the courage and the will to undertake the pilgrimage to that Promised Land. Unlike Carter's Serving strategy, which sought to listen to people's anxieties and support them, King's was a Visionary strategy, which stirred the hearts and minds of those around him.

What the Visionary strategy can achieve

The RSX strategy often has to make use of subversive tactics: without access to the channels of authority, it exercises influence through protest and catalysis. This Visionary strategy offers people another way, an alternative to the one they have hitherto taken as read. It begins by questioning the assumption that things cannot be different, and it asks: 'What would the world look like if we rewrote the script, if we tore up the rule book and started again?' In many organizations, imagination has simply been squashed over years of mundane productivity. Creativity quickly drains away unless it is fed and fostered. Some organizations simply lack the leadership to imagine a different world—to believe there could be another solution to their sales problem, or a different way to tackle the difficulties in their supply chain, or a new approach to 'people development'.

The RSX strategy also seeks to reform the language that followers use about themselves. Most people have an inbuilt resistance to something novel, which destabilizes the old and the familiar. 'Better the devil you know...' 'If it ain't broke, don't fix it'—this is the language of the weary manager, tired and cynical about new initiatives that promise much and deliver little. There has been a growing realization over the past 50 years that the language a leader uses to describe his role, his work, the organization in which he leads, has more power than he may be aware of. If you talk to someone who is depressed, for example, they may talk a lot about things being grey or black, about feeling trapped and powerless, unable to move forward. The language they use doesn't merely reveal how they see and feel about the world they inhabit—it's as if they are actually defining the colour and size and shape of that world.

I can remember a sustained period of depression I myself suffered. If you had asked me then to describe myself, I would have struggled to find positive words. My wife helped me one day to think about the impact of the negative images of myself that I lived with, and in a sense gave life to. She suggested that I needed to put these to death and bring to life instead some new, more affirming ways of speaking about myself. I began to try, writing down some positive statements about myself as a man, a father, a husband, a leader. I found that, gradually, I started to *inhabit* this new language about myself. Instead of being hunched, dishevelled and scowling, I began to walk tall, dress smartly, look people in the eye once more and believe in myself. The language slowly changed me.

King offered black Americans a new language in which to think of themselves. His speeches did more than merely stir emotions: they reinvigorated cowed and crushed imaginations, opening up broad horizons and depicting strong and noble shoulders ready and able to bear the weight of power and responsibility. Churchill, too, had his Visionary side, and his early war speeches provide a powerful and familiar example of this 'world-absorbing' power of speech in leadership. In the dark days of 1940, he used language to redefine the reality of millions of fearful folk gathered round their wireless sets. It was vital that he should project a version of reality opposed to the one that all the evidence set against them, and this he did, not by denying that evidence but by confronting it and also transforming it. The threat of invasion was something not to make them cower but to inspire resilience, resolve and courage. This island was portrayed as the last bastion of hope for the free world, standing alone against a terrible enemy. Churchill knew that ambivalence would be fatal—that if people were to accept the suffering that lay in store, they would need to see themselves in heroic terms, as engaged in a great struggle against dark powers. To create this perception, Churchill drew on the ancient Anglo-Saxon vocabulary at the heart of the English language. Thus the RSX leader sees herself as a storyteller or dramatist whose job is to create, with her audience, a world that is captivating, robust and compelling.

What, then, must a leader do in order to remodel reality for her followers? First, she must see her words as not merely informing but *transforming*. Second, she must invite people to participate in the drama of history. It's not inappropriate to use the word 'drama' in relation to leadership.[8] The leader

---

[8] Paul Ricoeur writes interestingly about the close relationship between metaphor and narrative in *The Rule of Metaphor: Multi-Disciplinary Studies of the Creation of Meaning in Language* (University of Toronto Press, 1977), trans Robert Czerny, pp19 and 24.

is a director who creates a piece of theatre in which she invites her followers to play their parts. She needs to be the one who draws the 'story arc' of the whole community. She may leave it to her cast to develop the script themselves, but she herself takes responsibility for the trajectory of the story. She must understand the characters and the themes and be aware of the moods, the threats, the climaxes. And she must explain to the cast the nature of the current scene, and how it relates to the bigger story.

More and more senior executives are becoming no more than bean counters, ministers of the spreadsheet, exegetes of the financial 'word'. They live in the prosaic language of financial reports, in thrall to the minutiae. This is a terrible price to pay for efficiency, because it robs organizations of the imagination, vision and perspective that characterize all great human endeavours. Many businesses have traded these for the levers of contractual controls, reward schemes and incentives.

When we appreciate the role of language in constructing our worlds, rather than merely reporting them, then it becomes clear that leadership is fundamentally about language. The words a leader uses are not simply a vehicle with which to convey information and deliver orders. Rather, his language itself creates the system of meaning in which the community functions and operates. So, for example:

- George W Bush uses the language of the cartoon strip to construct a black-and-white world of 'good guys' and 'bad guys' that legitimates his foreign-policy agenda.
- A corporate executive may speak in terms of execution, delivery, re-engineering and deployment—imagery derived from the world of systems and mechanics—to construct a system of meaning around the core values of reliability, performance and control.
- A politician may talk of empowerment, sharing, value and vision—metaphors that refer back to the world of the tribe—to construct a system of meaning around the core values of loyalty and responsibility.

A leader who employs the Visionary strategy examines carefully the imagery she uses. Many leaders simply adopt metaphors that are 'given' them by current social discourse, like people who dress shabbily in hand-me-downs or clothes picked up at jumble sales; but genuine progress—let alone transformation—rarely occurs without the adoption of a new vocabulary.

The reaction to the action

In creating a new vocabulary and a new vision, the leader also creates, almost accidentally, a new 'called-out' community, as people start to hear, learn and 'live' the new language. In the ecology of power, the corollary of the RSX strategy is PWC, as followers experience a sense of belonging together. In part, this is because they are distinguished by their differences from the wider community: they believe in a different message, a different gospel. There is always a sense of community when you feel embattled—and when a group of people hold radically different beliefs, the private world it creates often gives them such a sense of identity and security that they're willing and able to do things their opponents would not think possible. Perhaps that's why those people who marched peacefully behind King or under his banner—both black and white—were ready to suffer the batons of the police.

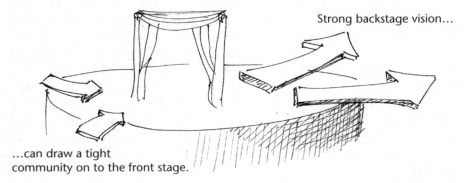

Strong backstage vision...

...can draw a tight
community on to the front stage.

This is also why those outside the movement feel so threatened. On 3 April 1968, King told a euphoric crowd: 'It really doesn't matter what happens now. ... Like anybody, I would like to live a long life. Longevity has its place, but I'm not concerned about that now. I just want to do God's will. And he's *allowed* me to go up to the mountain! And I've looked over, and I've seen the Promised Land. I may not get there with you. But I want you to know tonight that we, as a people, will get to the Promised Land. And so I'm happy tonight. I'm not worried about anything. I'm not fearing any man. Mine eyes have seen the glory of the coming of the Lord!'

Those words were to prove prophetic. The very next day, he was shot dead in his hotel room in an assassination that many believe may have been orchestrated by the FBI. His death provoked a wave of riots across America, but it also paved the way for an unstoppable revolution in civil rights for black Americans.

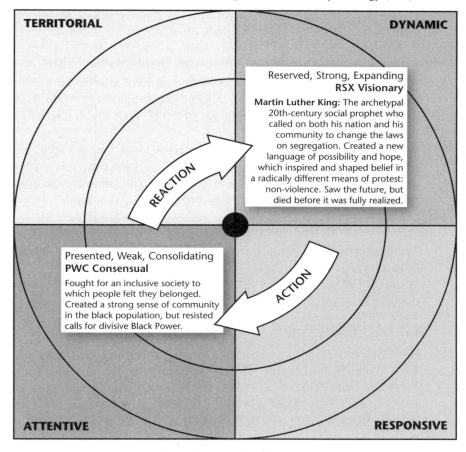

Diagram 11.1: Visionary (RSX) action and PWC reaction

How does a leader implement an RSX strategy?

There are four key elements to implementing this strategy effectively:

1. Highlight the current problems without providing premature solutions

- Most vision is born out of pain and dissatisfaction with the status quo. Allow discontent to brew.
- Help people to focus on current problems rather than simply papering over them.
- Allow unresolved issues to remain so and let others take responsibility for solving them.

· Wait until people are coming to you for a way forward before suggesting your solution.

2. Provide opportunities to dream dreams and explore possibilities

· At the beginning of a new project, once you have introduced it, you might ask members of the team to think of all the things they might want to know by the end. This can be a way of letting their minds wander to big ideas and exciting possibilities.
· Ask them to imagine all the things they could do if they learned how to (for example) run a training course—such as teach others to master a skill, win greater recognition and better rewards, influence the way things are done in the company or be better organized at home.

3. Provide vocabulary that will redefine people's current horizons

· Consider carefully the language you use. Examine the current vocabulary of your organization for its colour, shape and texture.
· If your organization were a kind of drama, what sort would it be? A soap opera? News programme? Factual documentary? Comedy? Tragedy? Fairy tale?
· Consider how clearly you see the overall 'story arc' of your organization.
· How confident are you that your cast appreciate it?
· What mechanisms do you have to communicate it to them?
· Consider how to reshape some of the language your organization uses, in order to convey a more compelling sense of the future you envisage.

4. Provide opportunities to build a sense of community—vision (RSX) is often closely related to belonging (PWC)

· Create a safe environment in which people can say anything without criticism.
· Respect every idea put forward.
· Suggest off-the-wall ideas yourself in order to model risk-taking. Make sure that some of your ideas can be improved on!

Some examples of RSX leadership in action

· A board choosing to double its investment in R&D
· A politician speaking in a campaign to reduce global poverty through fair trade
· A poet writing a ballad of love and remembrance

- A teacher capturing his students' imagination with his tales from history
- An engineer devising a new technology to improve a medical procedure
- A pharmaceutical company developing a new anti-cancer drug over seven years of research
- A priest inspiring followers, through his teaching of the Bible, to greater devotion and love

When to use an RSX strategy

- When more of the same is not going to change things for the better
- When structural forms of power are not available to you
- When people lack vision, hope and momentum
- In the face of a challenge or threat it will take courage and sacrifice to survive

TWELVE

Nelson Mandela and the Consensual Strategy (PWC)

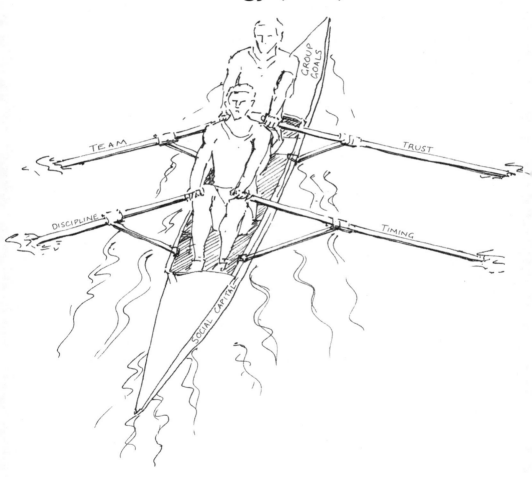

There is no doubt that Nelson Mandela will leave his mark on the imagination of a generation around the world. For many, it's remarkable enough that a man who had endured 27 long years in prison—mostly doing hard labour on

Robben Island—emerged unbroken. Others are profoundly impressed by his ability to go beyond recrimination and retaliation to find a more peaceful way. For others, he simply represents a symbol of fortitude and hope in the face of the darkness of human wickedness.

Mandela was born in the black 'homeland' of Transkei on 18 July 1918. His Xhosa name Rolihlahla could be taken to mean 'troublemaker,' a connotation that was to prove prophetic. Like King's, his country was racially segregated, under a policy of apartheid (Afrikaans for 'separation') adopted in 1948. People were classified as white, black, Indian or coloured (that is, mixed-race) and on that basis were kept apart from each other. In particular, black people (who constituted the great majority of the population) were legally citizens of various 'homelands' which were nominally sovereign nations but in fact were more akin to the Native American reservations or Australia's aboriginal reserves. In effect, this deprived non-white people of the vote (and other polical influence), as it restricted their rights to a distant territory they might never even have visited.

Like King, Mandela's political roots lay in protest. Believing that peaceful opposition was the best strategy, he joined the Youth League of the African National Congress and became involved in programmes of passive resistance to the laws that required blacks to carry passes and kept them in a state of permanent servility. However, in 1956 the South African government tried 156 of its principal opponents in the ANC for treason, and Mandela was among them. The trial dragged on for five years and ended in the acquittal of every one of the defendants—but by then the country had witnessed the massacre of peaceful black demonstrators at Sharpeville in 1960 and unrest was spreading. The government was intent on crushing all opposition, and most liberation movements, including the ANC, were banned.

Perhaps this was a turning point for Mandela. In 1961, he became the leader of the ANC's armed wing, which he had co-founded. He co-ordinated a campaign of sabotage against military, government and civilian targets, and planned for a possible guerrilla war if this failed to bring an end to apartheid. Now the most wanted man in South Africa, he was on the run for more than a year, so elusive the police nicknamed him 'the Black Pimpernel'. For a while he went abroad to enlist support for the ANC; but on his return he was arrested and sentenced to five years' hard labour for 'inciting African workers to strike' and 'leaving the country without valid travel documents'.

Within a matter of weeks, Mandela was dragged from prison to be charged with 'complicity in over 200 acts of sabotage aimed at facilitating violent revolution and an armed invasion of the country'. If convicted, this time he faced almost certain death. In the courtroom, he made a statement that would change the way he was perceived throughout the country: 'During my lifetime I have dedicated myself to the struggle of the African people. I have fought against white domination, and I have fought against black domination. I have cherished the ideal of a democratic and free society in which all persons live together in harmony and with equal opportunities. It is an ideal which I hope to live for and to achieve. But, if needs be, it is an ideal for which I am prepared to die.'

Mandela found that this stand gave him moral authority and he began to assume the leadership of the movement. His response to the ordeal of incarceration on Robben Island was to encourage his fellow prisoners to educate themselves. As they left their cells each morning to toil in the quarries, buffeted by the merciless southeaster or broiled by the sun, each team was assigned an instructor, in history, economics, politics, philosophy or whatever. In this way, their minds and spirits were sustained and enriched, despite the privations they were suffering. Two decades later, Mandela began a long and laborious attempt to negotiate directly with the South African regime. Now one of the most famous prisoners in the world, he was escorted, in the greatest secrecy, to the office of President F W de Klerk, where the two men began to prepare for the transition from apartheid to full democracy. On 2 February 1990, de Klerk lifted the ban on the ANC and announced Mandela's imminent release.

What followed was a battle in diplomacy. Mandela first had to secure the support of his own followers, and then had to address the far more difficult task of winning the trust of the white population. In that effort, Mandela's obvious integrity, combined with the wisdom and moral authority he had acquired over the years of suffering patiently endured, gave his voice power and credibility. But he still needed to have a heart that was big enough to forgive injustice, to lay the foundations for a new nation.

One of the key themes to which Mandela returned throughout his own presidency was the country that South Africans of all colours had been given to share. The unity of the nation was based on their common relationship with the land that lay beneath their feet. 'To my compatriots, I have no hesitation in saying that each one of us is as intimately attached to the soil of this beautiful country as are the famous jacaranda trees of Pretoria and the mimosa trees of the bushveld. Each time one of us touches the soil of this land, we feel a sense of personal renewal. ... That spiritual and physical oneness we all share with this common homeland explains the depth of the pain we all carried in our hearts as we saw our country tear itself apart in a terrible conflict, and as we saw it spurned, outlawed and isolated by the peoples of the world, precisely because it has become the universal base of the pernicious ideology and practice of racism and racial oppression.'

These words, taken from Mandela's inaugural presidential address, speak of the land as something living to which people belong in life as well as death. To the European or American mind, the language is quite foreign—we tend to think of land as inanimate, a thing to be owned and exploited. In the African paradigm, people and land are far more closely bound together in a single life. The identity of one people is conjoined with the identity of one land; the rupture of racism caused so much pain because it tore the land apart and violated its fundamental unity.

Such convictions about the very nature of shared society and the bonds that both hold it together and make it distinct, lie at the very heart of the PWC strategy of Consensual leadership—presented, weak and consolidating. This kind of power implies the choice *not* to use strong forms of force: not to exploit or to dominate. It implies a willingness to settle in one place, rather than expand relentlessly wherever you can. There is a commitment in it to the wellbeing, integrity and value of the place you find yourself in. It is in marked contrast to the PSX Pacesetting strategy, which seeks to dominate, expand and possess. It is also in contrast to the PSC Commanding strategy, which seeks to control, contain and conform. It is in contrast, too, to the PWX Affiliative strategy, which seeks to motivate and move on with restless energy.

You might look at Consensual leadership and feel at once how weak and fragile it is. At first glance, it seems to lack the will to dominate, the force to control. It lacks the drive to expand and take more. It feels like a more gentle, self-effacing and fundamentally *collective* approach. In this regard, it is highly non-Western. Fundamental to the Western enterprise, built as it is on the intellectual foundations of the Renaissance and the Enlightenment and shaped by the economic principles of the Industrial Revolution, are the values of ownership, opportunity and growth. Capitalism is merely the economic expression of a more innate human drive to consume. Individual rights (as opposed to collective responsibilities) and personal freedom (as opposed to communal commitment) lie close to the heart of most Westerners' ideology.

In contrast, the essence of the PWC strategy is to build up the strength of the relationships between people. My first boss, the pastor of a sizeable church, used to say to visitors who were wondering whether or not to join the congregation, 'What you need to do is to look at the spaces between people.' They would look at him, bemused for a moment until the penny dropped. Then they got it: the health and strength of the church—and of any organization, for that matter—lay not in the capacity of any one of its people or its departments, or in its vision or its growth, but in the strength of the bonds that existed between people. 'Look at the spaces between people'—that's how you can tell whether this is a community you want to be part of.

What the Consensual strategy can achieve

PWC leadership is all about strengthening the 'spaces' between people. In technical terms, this is what is known as 'social capital'. We are all familiar with the idea of financial capital, and probably know about intellectual capital; 'social capital' expresses the notion that a community's wealth lies not just in people's pockets or their brains but in their relationships—their trust of and commitment to one another.

Imagine, for example, an organization that has little social capital. You would find that people talked to each other only when they had to. Conversation around the coffee machine would be sparse and often negative, cynical and bitchy. This would be a place where rumours flew around and where if people could get out of a job, or get away with a half-truth, or pass the buck so someone else got the blame, they would. Teams would invariably be tense and often ineffectual, because their members were suspicious of each other, distrusting each other's motives and disrespecting each other's skills. At the time, you would sense that the real game was about individuals climbing up the ladder rather than about people working together to make the whole organization more productive and more fulfilling. This is the kind of organization I myself would avoid like the plague. No matter what business it was engaged in, no matter how much money it was making, or what its share value was, or what salary it was offering, it would be an utter misery to work for. My motivation, my concern, my energy would plummet. They wouldn't get the best out of me—and I'm sure they wouldn't get the best out of the rest of their staff, either.

On the other hand, imagine an organization that was the opposite in every respect. When you walked in, you were greeted with smiles and hellos. People enjoyed hanging out at lunch because the company was good and the mood upbeat. It wasn't uncommon to hear of one staff member offering help to another. Ideas were shared and people were valued and respected. Because it had a culture of trust, people took on responsibility because they weren't afraid of failing; and when someone got something wrong, they were helped to get it right next time. At every level, people were learning. In their teams they enjoyed support, exploration and discovery. People took the view that if the organization as a whole flourished, they as individuals would flourish, too. They saw that their interests were not in competition with their colleagues' but in harmony with them.

Now, that is the kind of organization I'd enjoy being part of. I suspect it would also get the best out of me. The difference between the two organizations is the quality of the spaces between people: the social capital of trust, concern and commitment based on the realization that the good of the individual is bound up inseparably with the good of all. This is the kind of organization that would be led by someone who used the PWC strategy. This strategy is not an expression of weakness (in the conventional, negative sense of the word); nor is it the product of a lack of vision, or of passivity and indecision, or of the leader's failure to take responsibility. Rather, it is a deliberate commitment to build the social capital of the organization, whether it be a business, a family, a government or a nation.

Often, such leadership involves considerable statesmanship and largesse: building up the strength of relationships in any meaningful way also involves 'decentring' and giving away power. If the organization is actually to be bound together, it takes more than people just being nice and friendly to each other. It also involves people genuinely trusting others, setting them free. In the days of apartheid, the weakness of South Africa, the drain in its social capital, lay not only in the overt hostility between whites and non-whites but also (and especially) in the legal restrictions that denied blacks both political influence and educational opportunity. It was the structure of power, which privileged a few at the expense of the many, that sapped both the legitimacy and the health of the country. For example, it wouldn't have altered the basic plight of a poor, disfranchised black South African simply to have enjoyed warm relations with a white neighbour; friendly banter, even hospitality, would not in itself have changed the fundamental, structural problem. The solution lay in both the transformation of personal relationships and the reconfiguration of legal and political relationships.

The statesmanship of the PWC leader, therefore, lies in his willingness to cultivate and embed structures that cede power and enable people to trust one another. For F W de Klerk, accepting the ANC and bringing an end to apartheid was to mean a loss of personal power. After he had made those changes, his presidency lost its legitimacy—he couldn't lead the new South Africa. The same can be said of the changes initiated by Mikhail Gorbachev in the Soviet Union: he made himself vulnerable in the process, and ultimately lost his very considerable power. For any authoritarian leader who embraces Consensual leadership, it will involve laying down the autonomy and control he once had and, instead, submitting to the discipline of being just one part of a much bigger, and ultimately stronger, whole.

For people who have suffered under such an autocratic regime, the way forward is the difficult path of forgiveness. When South Africa hosted the Rugby Union World Cup in 1995, it was the first time the country had been invited even to participate in the event, after the lifting of a ban imposed throughout the years of apartheid. The South African rugby team (known as the Springboks) had been made up exclusively of whites; it had a symbol of everything apartheid stood for and as such was hated by the black population. Mandela encouraged non-white South Africans to support the team, and after the Springboks had won an epic final against New Zealand, he wore a Springbok shirt to present the trophy to the captain, Francois Pienaar, an Afrikaner. This was widely seen as a major step forward in the reconciliation of white and black South Africans.

Of course, there are countries whose transformations have been less peaceful and successful than the transition from apartheid government to full democracy in South Africa. In the former Soviet Union, the instability that has ensued in regions such as the Caucasus illustrates graphically (and tragically) how difficult it is for a once dominating PSC government to reallocate power in a stable, non-authoritarian system. Much the same is true of the component parts of the former Yugoslavia. More often than not, factions and ethnic groups, previously bound together by a common hatred of their rulers but prevented from overthrowing it, find it hard, once they are free and empowered, not to see each other as the new enemy. The temptations afforded by the acquisition of power and the opportunity to dominate have proved too strong and have led to civil wars and other catastrophes. Of course, the ecology of power predicts that, when the lid of PSC Commanding power is removed, those who have suffered under its rule, suppressed as an RWX Servant population, tend to adopt the style of their oppressors. The challenge of establishing a culture of forgiveness and reconciliation after decades of violence and abuse is a monumental one that calls on all the resources of human goodness.

The story of post-Soviet Russia is just as distressing in its way as the tragedy now unfolding in Iraq. In the political chaos that followed the dismantling of the Communist regime, a few businessmen managed to seize economic power, taking control of the country's mineral and energy assets through a series of shady deals. The failure of a naive young democracy to create a robust legal structure to safeguard its new open markets allowed them essentially to steal most of the country's wealth before its very eyes. In political terms, democracy is the primary means to make a society strongly Consensual, as it ensures that each individual is recognized and empowered; but in Russia it has not been a success. The country is notionally democratic but the redistribution of power has been very patchy, on account of both the strength of the oligarchs and the readiness of the government to exercise authoritarian (PSC), rather than consensual (PWC), power.

In the West, while we may recognize that democracy is the best way to achieve a fair distribution of political power, we tend to make rather different assumptions about power structures in organizations. We're familiar with the top-down dynamic of control, from the board to the workforce (the trade union is the PWC counterbalance to this). However, more imaginative and collaborative systems have also proved successful. For example, Alcoholics Anonymous is an organization of about two million members, working in many languages and cultures right around the globe—yet it is staffed almost entirely by volunteers. It has, in its own words, 'no real government': every group is self-sufficient and decides its own ways of working, rules and customs. Nonetheless, it is a highly cohesive community. What binds it together, of course, is its members' shared experience of alcoholism, and their common commitment to the 'Twelve Steps' programme.

AA doesn't ask or accept money for its services, but such structures can also generate profitable businesses. I have already told the story of Linux in the first book of this trilogy, *Leading out of Who You Are*, but let me recapitulate it briefly. Linux is an alternative computer operating system, a competitor to the likes of Microsoft's Windows. Unlike Windows, however, Linux is freeware: you can download it onto your PC—or a whole officeful of PCs—absolutely free of charge. The reason is that every single line of its code was written by volunteers. It was the brainchild of a Norwegian called Linus Torvalds, who wrote the first code himself and then in 1991 invited other programmers to add to it. Since then, hundreds of thousands of lines of code have been contributed: none of the authors has been paid, and no one owns the copyright. The way the company behind Linux makes money is by selling support services to the organizations that use the software. By 2008, it is expected that Linux will have more than 37 per cent of the market. The basis of the whole operation is trust—the willingness of Torvalds to trust his contributors and of them to trust him, and of the public to trust both. This is particularly effective because all alike probably share a *dis*trust of (and even hostility towards) the domination of the field by Windows, to which Linux is seen as a radical, subversive alternative. This is the common vision: to create something that works on entirely different principles—technological, social and even moral—from those of the traditional market.

An even more high-profile example of a PWC organization that is both very productive and very profitable is eBay. At first glance, it seems a ludicrous idea to set up an online market in which people part with money for goods they haven't seen and have no guarantee of ever receiving from vendors who may be on the other side of the world and who may not even have the goods they are offering for sale. However, eBay has been a phenomenal success—and it depends entirely on trust. Does this mean, therefore, that all those who buy and sell on eBay are intrinsically more trustworthy than other people? Of course, the answer is almost certainly no: they are just as dishonest, just as willing to abuse the system, as anyone else. The reason they don't is that eBay has put in place a set of restraints that penalize people who have shown themselves to its virtual community to be untrustworthy. It all relies on feedback. Each time a sale is made, the buyer and seller are asked to rate each other's reliability, and in this way regular traders acquire a score that is visible to everyone. The system is thus self-sanctioning: you may find it profitable once to break faith, but you will reduce your credibility as a trader and this will make it harder for you to profit in the future. The social bonds ('the space between people') are so arranged as to discourage deceit and create a market that costs little to participate in and requires very few legal controls.

In all three of these examples, certain conditions were necessary to achieve a profitable distribution of power. A mechanism was needed whereby information and goods could change hands: for Linux and eBay this was the Internet, for AA the multiplication of small groups. The 'product' itself must be 'open-source' (or what has been termed 'copyleft'): rather than being copyright-protected, it must be freely available to anyone both to use it and to develop it. Each of my three examples represented a move away from initiatives driven and controlled by leaders towards leader/follower collaborations. In the former, a 'leader' decides the direction and both the desired and the actual outcomes of an enterprise; in the latter, he creates the conditions for the 'followers' to participate and share control. In order to effect this, a leader must be able to achieve two things that AA, Linux and eBay all achieved. The first is a vital idea that the community will share and safeguard. For AA, this was the Twelve Steps programme. For Linux, it was what Torvalds calls its 'kernel', the core of the code around which all the rest is built. For eBay, it was the profit motive. The second is a 'brand story' that is big enough and compelling enough to motivate those who take part to join in writing the storyline themselves. Finally, the leader must adopt management structures that allow followers to participate in directing the enterprise. The operation needs to incorporate feedback mechanisms that enable it to evolve and allow those who administer it to learn from what its co-creators are saying.

The reaction to the action

The reaction to the use of PWC power that is predicted by the ecology of power is RSX: reserved, strong and expanding, the domain of the visionary. One thing you notice about instances of PWC leadership and the structures rich in social capital they produce is that they are always funded by a powerful vision. Think of the kibbutz, an example of communal living based on sharing and collaboration. Behind this is a vision of what human society could be like—which is why many people enter a kibbutz for a period to have their own vision of society renewed. Again, a monastic community is always based on the spiritual vision of its founder, whether it be Francis, Benedict, Dominic or another 'saint'. Or, again, take a Western democracy such as France, whose social cohesion derives from a secular vision established in the Revolution.

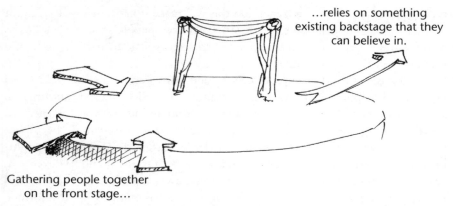

...relies on something existing backstage that they can believe in.

Gathering people together on the front stage...

In other words, a prerequisite for the formation of a PWC community rich in social capital is a deep ideological root that feeds the organization that grows out of it. Those PWC structures that fail to nurture their roots begin to lose the vision that funds them and gradually lose their social cohesion, drifting from social cohesion towards individualism. This is something we are witnessing in the West, where the loss of social and spiritual vision that has followed the decline in influence of the Christian faith has meant that arguably our democracies are slowly withering. Our commitments to social responsibility, freedom of speech and so on are becoming less strongly defended, and this has only accelerated the fragmentation of our societies.

Essentially, the vision that must inform a PWC strategy and underwrite its values is one of a common humanity, that sees people as equally human, possessing equal worth and dignity. No other vision will prove strong enough to withstand our tendency to sectarianism. This was the vision, funded by theology and faith, that inspired Martin Luther King's appeal for desegregation. No less, it was the vision that shaped Mandela's conception of South Africa post-apartheid. One day, when he was asked to comment on the BBC's somewhat unflattering verdict on his performance as a political leader, Mandela replied simply with a smile and a wry comment that expressed his deepest convictions about life: 'It helps to make you human.' At heart, what he believed in was the human spirit that binds us all together.

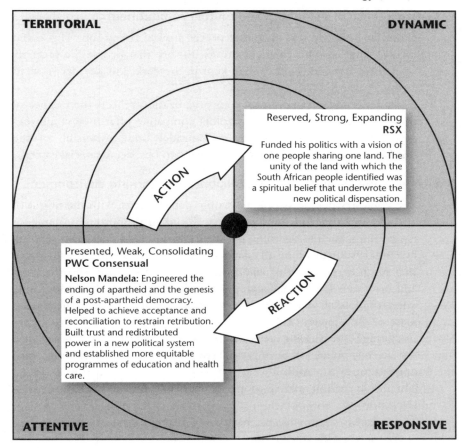

Diagram 12.1: Consensual (PWC) action and RSX reaction

How does a leader implement a PWC strategy?

There are four key elements to implementing this strategy effectively:

1. Work to overcome divisions and build trust

- Pay attention to any experiences of distrust, anger or sectarianism in your organization.
- Address it early by listening to the different points of view.
- Bring opposing sides together and help them to listen to each other.

2. Create a sense of belonging and mutual commitment

· Consider how you can distribute power around the group. This could involve rotating who chairs meetings. Ensure that people are properly briefed on key issues rather than kept in the dark. Put key decisions to a vote.

· Consider how the structure of your organization reflects the balance of power. For example, many shareholder companies offer their employees very little in the way of power. Consider how ownership of the organization could be distributed formally to best accrue social capital.

3. Establish, model and nurture a collaborative learning environment

· You could try pairing people up within departments, with the object of enabling them to work collaboratively. (Think of an appropriate name for the pairings, such as 'learning partners'.) You would find that everyone benefited from this kind of 'peer' mentoring and support. You would also see how gifted some people are in nurturing others in this way, and how well some 'challenging' individuals respond. Remember how effective Mandela's 'Island University' was in engaging and educating so many of the inmates on Robben Island.

· Encourage the sharing of ideas. Most adults learn best when they are actively engaged in a task. When teaching or presenting, take opportunities to enable the group to participate as much as possible. This could include asking people to face their partners to do some of the following:

  Explain to them what *you* have just explained

  Share some ideas

  Test each other on how well they understand what you have just said

  Think of examples to illustrate the point you have just made

  Work out a problem. Have a flip chart available during meetings on which anyone can write any idea or suggestion.

4. Deliberately incorporate some activities that require collaborative thinking or work

· It's very interesting to watch how different individuals respond to collaborative learning experiences. You will see people playing a variety of roles, from taking the lead to opting out. The most valuable part of such an activity is helping them afterwards to reflect on what happened.

· This can help people to learn skills such as listening to another perspective, overcoming difficulties, managing conflict and so on.

- As a leader, your role is not only to enable people to do a task but also to nurture (and equip them to develop) their confidence, independence and ability to learn.

Some examples of PWC leadership in action

- A community or population embracing democratic structures that give political recognition to the value of each individual
- A committee adopting consensual chairing and putting decisions to the vote
- A family sitting around the meal table discussing what they are going to do the next day
- A trade union giving individual workers a more powerful, collective voice
- A peacemaker in the family, who listens and is warm, smoothing over differences and reducing tensions so that warring parties can listen to each other

When to use a PWC strategy

- When faced with an unstable situation, where bridges need to be built and things in common found
- Where trust is low
- As a way of limiting the top-down exercise of power and preventing its abuse
- To spread ownership of a project or organization
- To encourage teamwork and foster a team spirit

THIRTEEN

Jesus and the Self-Emptying Strategy (RWC)

For many, the death of Jesus of Nazareth some two thousand years ago was a tragic martyrdom. They look at the life of this remarkable man and think how sad it was that it was ended so early, while he was still in his thirties. He had so much more to offer: he could have achieved so much more, shared so much more wisdom. Some people also wonder wistfully whether, had he lived a bit longer, his followers might have grown to be a little more like him, for in their experience the church his disciples established seems very different in character from the life and teaching of the man who inspired them.

From the perspective of social history, Jesus was a victim. His execution was ordered by an insecure Roman governor, Pontius Pilate, under pressure from an envious Jewish elite who judged the rabbi from Galilee to be a threat to their leadership and control. It is only those who follow the man as his disciples who see his death in other terms. They agree that those who had Jesus killed were culpable for his execution—which, indeed, was entirely unjustified by the false charges brought against him. However, they also maintain that his death was no accident, no mistake. They argue that Jesus died *willingly*—that he had had plenty of opportunity to escape from those who were coming to arrest him. Moreover, it appears that he consciously and intentionally put himself in the way of death, and predicted it would happen. Not only did he 'volunteer' to die, he also taught from early on in his ministry that his dying would be an act that, in itself, would release power—God's power—and would transform the social and spiritual order. In other words, he saw his death not as an occasion of weakness and defeat but as his most powerful display of strength. He saw it not as the end of his vision but as its beginning. He saw it not as a capitulation to powers he could not overcome but as his overthrowing of them.

Indeed, if you consider the impact of Jesus' life in comparison with the impact of what ensued after his death, there would seem to be some truth in his prediction. In his lifetime, he travelled no more than a few hundred miles from his birthplace; within 50 years of his death, the message he had been proclaiming had reached thousands of miles, to north Africa, Spain and possibly even India. In his lifetime, he addressed an almost exclusively Jewish audience; since his death, his message has been embraced by people of almost every race and has been translated into many hundreds of languages and dialects. In his lifetime, he inspired a few hundred people to follow him; by his death, he has inspired hundreds of millions to do so, thousands of whom have given their lives for their faith.

Many people have regarded Christianity as a death cult—as the veneration of a murdered saint, or the worship of the dying god. This misses the point, however. The power of Jesus' death doesn't lie in some macabre embrace of death itself, in some dark gothic fantasy; rather, it lies in what Jesus' followers say his death made possible: life. Christians see the death of Jesus as an act that brought life. Their celebration of his death is, in fact, a celebration of the life that flows from it. The veneration of Jesus on Good Friday, the day on which traditionally Christians remember his death, is followed two days later by the celebration of Easter Sunday, when they rejoice in what they believe to have been his resurrection from the grave.

This narrative of death and resurrection is a captivating tale of triumph in the face of disaster, of strength in the face of weakness and of gain in the face of loss. It speaks to the deepest needs of the human heart. The one reality from which we cannot escape is death—our own as well as that of those we love, which robs us of all we hold dear. Death represents the ultimate loss, the final confirmation of human impotence. If we are to find a satisfactory account of power, we must try to explain this experience of total weakness. Conventionally, death is perceived as the annihilation of power—both the annihilation of someone *by* power and the annihilation *of* power in the one who is dead. The death-and-resurrection narrative, however, calls this formula into question: it suggests not only that death itself may be robbed of power but that the power available in the life that follows death is greater than that available in the life that precedes it.

How can any of this possibly be true? The burial or cremation of tens of thousands of people this very day seems to confirm the finality of death and its extinction of all that was once alive. This is certainly true. I am not for a moment suggesting that some great cosmic reversal is in train by which, through some magician's trick, all death is turned into life. I do believe in a resurrection, both spiritual and physical; but I am not primarily talking about such a thing here. I am instead talking about how power *within the human sphere* can be released through the sacrifice of life.

Think, for example, of the power of the martyr. When a righteous man or woman gives their life for their cause, it is inspirational. Most religions venerate those who have died for the cause in the face of unjust persecution. If we broaden the term a little, we could regard as martyrs those Indians who peacefully marched in the cause of Independence and were clubbed to the ground. We could regard as martyrs the marchers who endured police brutality and imprisonment during the American Civil Rights movement. We could consider those people imprisoned for their faith in countries that restrict religious freedom: in China, Burma, Saudi Arabia, North Korea and much of the former Soviet Union. We could consider political prisoners who have refused to submit to tyrannous regimes. The word 'martyr' literally means 'witness': one who bears witness to the truth through his blood, his body, his loss.

What all these people seem to have in common is the weakness in which they confronted a system that was both strong and morally repugnant. Now, it appears that, under certain circumstances, this imbalance—the weakness of one against the immoral strength of the other—can bring about a radical shift in power. Without doubt, it was reports of this kind of situation that eroded the moral authority of the British Raj and precipitated negotiations towards an independent India. Without doubt, it was images of such a situation that shook America in the 1960s and turned the tide in favour of desegregation. Without doubt, it was such a situation that drained the moral credibility and political will of the apartheid regime in South Africa.

How can this be? How can power be located in such displays of weakness? How can vulnerability work to change the course of events? Here is one answer: self-sacrifice can draw out the evil of the enemy. As long as Indians resisted the British with force, it could be argued that the British had a right to beat them down. However, when Indians did not use any force and did not resist, when they took the blows of the rifle butts and batons on their heads, any right the British had evaporated. Indeed, the authorities' readiness to use brutal measures to suppress peaceful opposition was exposed for all to see. Previously, it had been hidden. Previously, their desire to dominate had been concealed backstage, while the front stage presented the well-mannered spectacle of tea and cucumber sandwiches. However, the self-sacrifice of the Indian marchers brought it out and revealed it.

Here is another answer: self-sacrifice compels people to take responsibility for their choices. As long as Indians used violence against the British, it was possible—even easy—for their fellow countrymen watching from the sidelines not to take sides. Why should they? Were armed insurgents a good thing? They seemed rather bloodthirsty—perhaps their rule would be worse than the British! Other Indians could remain uncommitted, while in Britain those who felt some pangs of conscience about the rule of the Raj would have been dissuaded from opposing it by reports of the violence of the natives. These people needed to be kept in check, they clearly couldn't rule themselves—they didn't have the moral discipline. However, when rifle butts and staves cracked the skulls of innocent, peaceful, white-clad men, young and old, the picture changed. The horror! The brutality! The unjustified suffering! This needed to be opposed, stopped! From that moment, a choice had to be made. Moral indecision was not an option.

Consider this, too: self-sacrifice compels people to take action. When a leader withdraws, she leaves a vacuum. As long as she is present, we can rely on her: she'll get us through this, we say, she'll come up with a plan, she'll sort this mess out! Strong power encourages complacency and apathy—there is too little incentive to take the reins ourselves. However, when that leader has gone, the issue becomes urgent. Of course we must act—no one else will! Either we do something or we suffer the consequences. Inaction is not an option.

Self-sacrifice is the conscious choice not to use force or to exercise power but instead to allow something to be done to *you*. Inevitably, therefore, it involves a degree of suffering and risk. It may be the emotional suffering of letting a loved one walk away, and the risk they may not come back. It may be physical suffering under persecution or even torture. In this regard, self-sacrifice is the weakest, most powerless course of action: unlike the other seven we have looked at, this final strategy—reserved, weak and consolidating—involves doing nothing, abdicating your right to impose yourself and choosing to allow others to impose on you. The combination of weak force and the drive to consolidate means that this kind of leadership is about leaving space for others to act. When it's employed deliberately, it obliges followers to take responsibility for their choices: there is a genuine withdrawal of the leader's presence that leaves his followers to cope without him. Direction, focus, authority are absent. The situation feels uncertain, tense, vacant—but also pregnant, awaiting a renewal of leadership. The leader allows others to come to the fore, to pursue their own initiatives, whatever the outcome. By renouncing active influence, he allows other leaders to emerge and accepts the risks associated with this lack of control.

What the Self-emptying strategy can achieve

It's important to recognize that I'm not referring here to the abdication of power as a dereliction of duty. The 'absent leader', the one who walks away, is very different from the Self-emptying leader. The former lets people down when they need support; the latter judges that the best and most powerful— and, indeed, most responsible—action is to choose not to exercise influence. The Self-emptying leader is, in one sense, fully engaged, fully present: this is a strategy that requires the utmost courage and determination, to restrain yourself even in the face of provocation.

It's important also to recognize that I'm not promoting suffering for its own sake. I see no good in pain and loss in themselves at all. They are merely tools with which we can achieve greater ends if we use them correctly. They are not an end in themselves—we progress through them towards an end where there will be no more death, or mourning or crying or pain.

What I am advocating is—on occasion—the strategic use of weakness, of self-emptying, in leadership. Just as there are situations in which each of the other seven strategies is appropriate, so there are situations in which the RWC Self-emptying strategy is right. I believe that several conditions need to be met if it is to be used wisely. First of all, the leader must be willing to suffer. You can't coerce someone else to suffer or it becomes an abuse of power. Self-emptying must be voluntary, informed and deliberate.

Second, the leader must be able to bear the suffering without being overwhelmed. King advised his followers not to march if they could not endure being struck by batons or water cannons without lashing out in retaliation.

It takes an extraordinary kind of discipline and maturity to absorb such provocation.

Third, it is wise to use this strategy only when there is a moral conscience to arouse and an emotional consciousness to be awakened in those who witness it. A recent, poignant illustration of this point was the suicide of the American musician Malachi Ritscher, who publicly burned himself to death during the rush hour in Chicago on 3 November 2006 in protest at the 'mass murder of innocent civilians' in Iraq. In his suicide note, he wrote that his countrymen were 'more concerned with sports on television and ring-tones on cellphones than the future of the world'. Unfortunately, his words proved to be prophetic, as his terrible end was almost completely ignored by the American media. He had expressed the hope that his one death could 'say to the world: I apologize for what we have done to you'—but it seems that no one was listening or had ears to hear him.

The reaction to the action

It is disturbing to think, even for a moment, that vulnerability may have something to contribute to leadership. We have been so indoctrinated with the received wisdom that we can't see past it: being a leader means being in control, being in power, having options, having information, having skills and resources. Leadership is not supposed to be about weakness and fragility and self-sacrifice. But what is extraordinary in the ecology of power is that power can flow through a point of weakness. In the moment of defeat, power can be released. So it was through the self-sacrifice of a few hundred Indian men, when the populace of the whole subcontinent, some 200 million men, women and children, were empowered to take control of their own lives. In the same way, the Christian church which was cruelly persecuted by the Roman emperors in the first and second centuries came to be more powerful than the Empire itself. This is the power of a wizened, bent old lady in the slums of Calcutta to challenge the hard-hearted assumptions of the world's economists. It is the power of Gorbachev to release the grip of Communism and allow a new order to emerge. It is the power of Gandhi to state that 'passive resistance is a method of securing rights by personal suffering.'

Leaders often say they are trying to 'do themselves out of a job'. By that, they are implying that if they do their work as leaders sufficiently well, their followers will be so well trained, equipped and empowered they'll be able to take on everything that needs to be done and they themselves will finally be redundant. This is an ideal of what you might call 'enabling leadership'. Certainly, there is some merit in this approach, which has grown out of the experience of many people that their leaders never relinquish control and so those who follow them never grow up fully and learn to take responsibility. Some leadership is still strongly paternalistic, with followers as dependants expecting their problems to be sorted out by a parent figure. In contrast, the enabling model encourages leaders to see themselves first of all as equippers of others: teachers who train others to be as competent as themselves, if not more so.

In the ecology of power, this kind of leadership is what you would call RSC or Foundational. It involves the laying of foundations, by providing resources, training, support—rehearsing the cast so that eventually the show can go on without the director. The assumption behind this is that independence is a good thing. The logic is that if a team or an organization fails to gain independence from its leader, it will always, in some ways, remain dependent on her—and so will be vulnerable should something ever happen to her. However, I'm not convinced that this kind of independence is ever entirely appropriate. There's a difference between being able to trust yourself and being so self-sufficient you no longer need anyone else. The former is certainly a mark of maturity, but the latter implies a lack of vulnerability, as well as a lack of maturity. No human being ever is, or should aspire to be, so self-sufficient they can do without the support and help of anyone else. That is a recipe for arrogant autonomy. The proper goal for leaders (and this includes parents) is not to make their dependants entirely self-sufficient, simply having no need of them, but to foster self-awareness and the ability to trust themselves as well as others.

There often comes a moment when a leader needs to 'let his followers go'. I have talked at length in the first book of this trilogy, *Leading out of Who You Are*, about the way followers can idealize a leader. Anyone who has led a community, an organization or a country for any length of time, through bad as well as good times, and remained faithful and humane will have formed a strong bond of affection with his followers. Moreover (as I pointed out in Chapter 3 of this book) they will see him as a symbol of their identity. The time will come, however, when this transaction must end—and the leader must help his followers to prepare for this. This is an act of mutual release, the letting-go of a relationship that has supported and sustained them on the journey they have made together. The role of the leader in this situation is to help his followers to navigate this emotional experience without being overwhelmed by it.

In the final months of his life, Jesus spoke often about his imminent death, as well as the resurrection that would follow. His disciples were confused and so he tried to elucidate, explaining why he needed to die and also foretelling what would happen next. The night before his execution, he enacted with his closest friends a ritual that has been imitated by his followers ever since. Sharing bread and wine around a meal table, mindful of the Jewish festival of Passover, which symbolized God's act of liberation from slavery, Jesus offered his disciples a rite by which to remember his own approaching sacrifice to free the world from slavery to sin. Today, Christians all around the world, of whatever denomination, re-enact this ritual: the Eucharist, Holy Communion, the breaking of bread, the Mass. In so doing, they share in those final hours of Jesus' life and prepare themselves to receive the benefits of his death and participate in the life he called people to as his disciples.

Jesus was preparing his followers for his final withdrawal, after which he would no longer be present with them. The time had come for him to 'let them go'—and for them to let him go. 'Don't hold on to me,' he told Mary Magdalene when she met him in the garden after his resurrection. Of course, his physical withdrawal made possible the greater release of his spiritual power, in the gift of his Holy Spirit, who Christians believe empowers the church for a self-sacrificial life of witness and worship.

Many leaders speak of 'enabling leadership', of 'doing themselves out of a job', and yet they fail to achieve this because they're not able to withdraw from their followers when the time is right. A leader can become an obstruction to confidence and growth if he stays too long, if too much is invested in him. The founder of the organization prevents growth after a while because everyone still 'sits under her authority', so to speak, even though they are unaware they're doing so. People defer to a founder and yield to a longstanding leader, and when her authority needs to be outgrown if the organization is to grow further, the only way it can happen is for the leader to withdraw: to empty herself as a final expression of her attachment to the thing to which she may have devoted her life. It is a little death, a loss, a giving-away, a hollowing-out. And yet for the followers she leaves behind, if it is done in a healthy and responsible way, it can lead to both freedom and empowerment.

Withdrawing from the stage altogether...

... may release powerful reactions, both for good and for bad.

The reaction to RWC leadership is PSX. The inverse of self-emptying is transforming. It seems that in the ecology of power an act of great weakness is linked to a release of great power—unexpected, dangerous, often uncontrollable power, power that no leader can teach or organize or buy. The reason self-emptying has such mighty effects is that in the ecology of power it produces the most potent reaction. It can galvanize the strongest of human emotions and drives. It has an energy and life of its own. There was no stopping what ensued in India in the early Forties. There was no stopping what ensued in America in the Sixties. There was no stopping what ensued in the Soviet Union in the Eighties. There was no stopping what ensued in South Africa in the early Nineties.

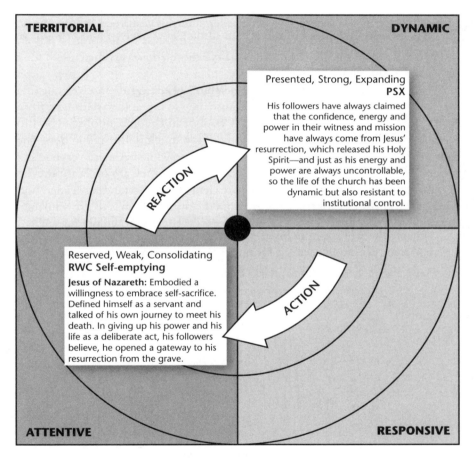

Diagram 13.1: Self-emptying (RWC) action and PSX reaction

Here are some examples of RWC leadership in action

- A chair withdrawing from a meeting to allow the rest of the board to come to a decision without her
- A politician choosing not to defend himself against some accusation or slander
- A mother allowing her teenage daughter to go to a party without saying what time she'll be back
- An army falling back in a show of weakness in order to deceive the enemy into thinking it's defeated
- A founder letting go of the organization she conceived and brought to birth

When to use an RWC strategy

- When faced with an unjust situation that needs to be exposed as such
- When you feel a call to sacrifice yourself in order to achieve a greater good
- When there is sufficient moral consciousness for your act to be recognized, so that it will catalyse change
- As a witness to injustice—which implies that the witness must be visible. For some, this may be simply in the sight of God; for others, it will mean while the world is watching.
- When revolution is called for rather than evolution
- As an act of solidarity with the weak

PART III

UNDEFENDED POWER

FOURTEEN

Finding the Holy Grail of Leadership

Eight different leaders, eight different leadership strategies. Each leader exemplifies the characteristics—strengths as well as weaknesses—of one of the strategies. Of course, none of these men was confined to using only that strategy: throughout his life and his career each would at times, in different situations, have used others. I have identified each strategy with a particular leader merely because they demonstrated it particularly powerfully.

It is also true that organizations—and, indeed, societies—go through different phases in which they look for different kinds of leadership. I have seen many organizations that, after the incumbency of one especially driven Pacesetting CEO, have appointed as his successor someone much more collaborative and Affiliative: following PSX with PWX leadership. Often, in such an appointment the organization is adjusting its internal balance after the impact of one particular character. It can also reflect the way that human communities have different needs at different times in their histories and look, often unconsciously, for leaders whose dominant strategies answer the needs they are conscious of at the time.

For example, Churchill's Britain was a country faced by an enemy of seemingly invincible might. His predecessor as prime minister, the emollient Neville Chamberlain, lacked the necessary bloody-mindedness to overcome such a challenge. Churchill's uncompromising personality, his indomitable bulldog spirit—indeed, his appetite for the battle—made him the kind of leader people craved and needed in 1940.

Margaret Thatcher's Britain was a different place. In 1979, this was a society struggling to escape the clumsy grip of the trades unions, which was stifling productivity and economic growth. For her, Britain was a country facing an 'enemy within', and so she appealed not to our common heritage but to our individualism. Thatcher tuned in to the message of the Sixties and Seventies, of the freedom of the individual, and gave it a political and economic interpretation. Her strident, Commanding PSC approach confronted the opposition and legitimated self-interest.

By the late 1990s, the British had had enough of the authoritarianism of Thatcher, the hypocrisy of the Conservatives and the instability of the economy. This was a society that wanted a new Affiliative sense of belonging. Tony Blair's language, manner and approach struck all the right chords to convince people that he offered a fresh start. His rhetoric was classic PWX: 'us' (rather than 'you'), 'our vision', 'our land', 'our time'. It was a positive, optimistic (if ultimately unrealistic) appeal to our sense that we wanted to be part of a vibrant new, emerging world.

Crucially, an effective leader resonates with his society—tuning into the same frequency, humming in the same key—and he exploits this. When this occurs, a relationship forms between the leader and his followers that binds the two together in a contract of trust and, for a while at least, the two become identified with each other. The strongest bonds between leaders and followers usually are formed when the social conditions are acute and so people's need to be made secure is greatest. When the social context is less extreme, the resonance and the bond between leader and followers are, inevitably, less strong.

The transition from one style of leadership to another is prompted, then, when this bond is broken—when the resonance that united leader and followers becomes a dissonance. Perhaps the most dramatic and shocking example in recent political history of such instant dissonance after a period of strong attachment is the effectual rejection of Churchill's government in the 1945 election. Churchill had been bound to the British people over the crucial war years by an emotional tie, because he was the symbol of their dogged resistance to the Nazi threat. However, in the early summer of 1945, following the end of the war in Europe and the break-up of the wartime coalition between Conservative, Liberal and Labour politicians, he called a general election. Despite overwhelming public affection for Churchill (whose approval rating only that May had been 83 per cent), despite predictions of a big win for his Conservatives, the Labour Party under the uncharismatic Clement Attlee was swept to power, winning almost two-thirds of the seats in the House of Commons.

The size of Churchill's defeat matched the strength of the tie that had bound him to the people through those extraordinarily demanding years of war. Once they were over, the need for that bond was past. Indeed, with Britain in ruins, the urgent need was for a government that was not identified with the hardships and sacrifices of the war but instead stood for progress, reconstruction and growth. In hindsight it seems almost inevitable that the man the people had clung to through the storm would not convince them that he could lead them in the aftermath. Churchill was never as great as a peacetime party politician as he was as a national leader and statesmen in wartime. His impassioned PSX rhetoric, drawing on the deep wells of the British spirit, was appropriate to the darkest of days when heroism and sacrifice were required, but was less suited to the moderate optimism of the careful social reconstruction needed after the war. The resonance had gone, and with it the political bond—though the emotional tie remained, and indeed ensured a return to No 10 for Churchill six years later. By 1951, of course, the welfare state (and especially the National Health Service) was well in hand and the reconstruction of Britain well under way, and people could again afford to recall their attachment to their great war leader. Even so, there was never again the same strong bond that had tied them together in the years 1940–45.

What becomes clear is that no single one of the eight leadership strategies is sufficient in itself. Each one achieves a particular effect, creates a particular configuration of power. What is important is whether a leader understands the kind of power she is using and whether it is the appropriate kind to use in that situation. For example, the parent who adopts a Consensual strategy when a child is about to run across the road in front of an oncoming car is using the wrong kind of power for that situation. The executive who employs a Commanding strategy when chairing a board of colleagues of similar status is using the wrong kind of power for that situation. The government that uses a Pacesetting strategy to drive a bill through Parliament is using the wrong kind of power in that situation. Leadership is not about being able to use any one form of power. It's not just about being able to create consensus, or face down opposition, or set a demanding pace. It's a bigger task than that.

Leadership itself must be thought of as a 'meta-activity'—that is, an activity that can see beyond any particular situation and has available to it a range of potential interventions, as well as the capacity to know when and how to implement them. Clearly, what matters is the repertoire of strategies a leader possesses. Each individual's 'signature' (so to speak) is the particular array of strategies he is able to use effectively to shape a situation. Every leader has such a signature, which identifies their presence and their social and emotional impact. Pope John Paul II, for example, used an affiliative PWX strategy very effectively, forming strong emotional bonds with people both through his travels and his displays of courage. He also sought to give the Catholic Church a vision, employing an RSX strategy—and after the attempt to assassinate him and towards the end of his life he also showed himself to be weak and vulnerable, a suffering leader who was pouring himself out for the church. However, he will not be remembered for his Pacesetting or Foundational approach.

Bill Clinton was known for his PWX and consensual PWC strategies. His foreign policy was more affiliative than that of either his predecessor or his successor, and in his own country he fostered a sense of openness. However, he, too, did little to reinforce the foundations of his society, relying instead on a relatively benign period of economic growth to create optimism at home.

George W Bush, on the other hand, has a leadership signature that is strongly slanted towards command and control. His rhetoric renders shades of grey in black and white and reduces complex issues to simple formulas in which the American people are the good guys and their enemies are the bad guys. His concept of international collaboration conjures up images of hospitality on his Texan ranch: 'Come and join me and the boys for a steak and a beer! We'll be rootin' out some cattle rustlers later if you stick around.' Confident, dominant, welcoming on his terms—in his policy he is almost exclusively PSC. It is because he's unable to employ other leadership strategies that his signature appears so perfunctory. It's not that a Commanding approach is inappropriate in itself, but on its own it becomes simplistic and dangerous.

Many leaders other than Bush lack this 'meta-leadership' ability. They are adequate, even effective, in one approach or another—they can practise Consensual leadership or Pacesetting leadership, perhaps—but they lack the mobility to progress beyond this to exercise a different kind of power when occasion demands. Mobility is the most important capacity a leader needs to develop. To some extent, this is something that can be learned—there are certain mechanics involved in moving from using one strategy, one kind of power, to another and you can master them. You can learn how to chair meetings in a Consensual way, for example—walking into the room and taking your seat with an air of confident authority. You can develop the ability to be warm and relational and Affiliative. You can learn, in short, to adopt different strategies as appropriate and use power to achieve different effects.

A very moving story that illustrates the potency of such mobility is that of the Guinea Pig Club. During the Battle of Britain, many pilots suffered appalling injuries when their fighters were hit by enemy fire and engulfed in flames. Reconstructive surgery was in its infancy in 1940, but some badly burned men were sent to the Queen Victoria Hospital in East Grinstead to be treated by the pioneering surgeon Archibald McIndoe, a man known to his colleagues as 'the Boss' or 'the Maestro'. The first batch of pilots decided to set up a club, which only men who had been patients at the burns unit could join, and called it 'the Guinea Pig Club' because they knew how experimental this surgery then was. MacIndoe encouraged this kind of humour as a way to deal with the trauma and stigma caused by their horrific injuries. (He himself liked to refer to these men as his 'boys'.)

Aware that many of his patients were going to spend a long time at the hospital—some of them had to undergo over 30 operations—McIndoe also got the East Grinstead community involved. Heroes or not, he knew that the pilots would not find it easy to mix with the townspeople, not only because of their disfigurement, which others would find it hard to look at, but also because of the intensity of all the experiences they had gone through. However, two good friends of his, Neville and Elaine Blond, managed to persuade some local families to take some convalescents into their homes as guests. Gradually, more and more people agreed to help, and in this way the pilots became integrated into the community. They soon became a familiar sight in the pub, and a number of them even married women they had met at dances organized by the Boss.

Everyone assumed that the Guinea Pig Club would disband when its members left the hospital at the end of the war, but six decades later it is still going strong and it meets every year for an emotional reunion. The Guinea Pigs speak of the way McIndoe restored their sense of dignity, their self-respect and their confidence. An extraordinary camaraderie has developed between them all, and many of these, now elderly, men will say that, despite the horror of their injuries, if they could have their life again they would not want to miss out on the experience of being members of the Club.

Few people can claim to have pioneered a new medical technique like McIndoe (who was knighted in 1947). Perhaps even fewer can claim also to have pioneered a kind of group therapy, long before the psychological revolution of the 1960s and some 60 years before such practices were to be used to address cognitive disorders in the NHS. McIndoe combined technical skill and imagination with an extraordinary insight into the emotional needs of men. At the same time, he had the vision to initiate, and the social skills to foster, a fellowship of humour, courage and adventure in a situation of terrible suffering and loss.

Sir Archie McIndoe was a man whose leadership signature was admirably fluent.

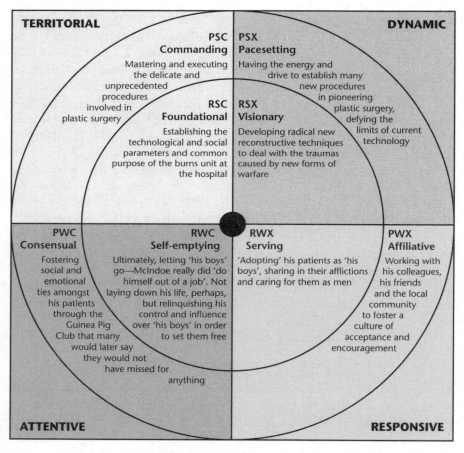

Diagram 14.1: The characteristics of McIndoe's leadership

The skills that enable mobility in leadership

1. Master each strategy

You can't employ a strategy unless you know when to use it. This is entirely a matter of competence. If we are not willing to train ourselves to be better leaders, we may as well give up now.

Using strong force. For example, you can't execute the PSC Commanding strategy unless you know how to gain and keep people's attention and respect, project authority and issue orders. This may be a matter of attending to your body language, your tone of voice and your behaviour around people. If we simply lack awareness of how we come across, we will need to enlist the help of others to give us some feedback about how we are thought of. Like mastering a new sports skill or a part in a play, this is to some extent a matter of learning the behavioural mechanics. When I first began to speak in public, I was nervous and tense, tied to my script. It took a while for me to learn the rhetorical and performance skills to practise Commanding or Pacesetting leadership from the front.

Language: An interesting exercise is to go through a talk, speech or presentation you're going to give and replace polysyllables with simple words. Illustrate often. Stick to the point, don't digress, be direct.

Symbols: Consider what symbols are associated with your 'message'. When you are speaking, the symbols around you will probably be speaking even louder: your clothes, your gestures and expressions, your poise, the way the room is set out, the lectern you lean on, the notes you give people, the welcome they received at the door, even the location of the venue. These things are not extra to your message, they are integral to it: they express it more powerfully than your words will, and they do so subliminally. How do you as a leader use symbolic language?

Gesture and movement: Do you have an understanding of gesture? Are you aware of how you stand, how you hold your papers when presenting? For example, the action of standing up in a group can indicate the taking of authority. Simply by standing up to seize people's attention as you introduce a new idea and then sitting down again to invite feedback and discussion, you can manage the emotional dynamics in the group. In the course of a meeting, I aim to stand up and then sit down five or six times. Or, again, I will employ some arm gestures to reinforce my point—for example, bringing my fingertips slowly together in front of me if I am talking about bringing a problem to a resolution, or throwing my arms wide to say that this idea is big enough to encompass the whole situation.

Often, I will try to use the whole room as a theatre, walking down from the stage to illustrate a point. If you begin making a proposal on one side of the room and slowly walk across to the other side as you fill in the detail, the gesture says: Here is something that can move you from A to B. I often look back across the room to my starting point and draw attention to how far I have come, step by step. I will always aim to make eye contact with each person in an audience of up to 20 or so as I talk. A speaker's task is to make people feel they are being addressed personally, and even momentary eye contact achieves this. I will always exaggerate my actions on stage, as if in a pantomime, because subtle gestures tend to be lost.

Resonance and the use of visual media: I personally believe that an active, energetic presentation, using gestures to echo meaning, is much more effective than PowerPoint. The latter restricts you to a linear flow and often reduces the theatre of the occasion. They are suitable for financial reports, where clear, informational charts are needed, but not good for other contexts.

The reason for this is that a good speaker achieves a resonance with her audience, so that the flow of her talk is determined not by a preset script but by the emotional connection between her and her audience. She becomes aware as she speaks of whether they are with her. When this point is reached, they are captivated and the atmosphere changes: an environment has been created in which her audience are sensitive to her. Their ears and hearts are open, they trust the speaker and she can begin to connect with their emotional needs. There is no foretelling exactly what language she will need at this point—she could not have prepared a text. All she can do is 'be still and listen to the space'.

Dramatic climax and timing: To be able to go off-script like this requires experience—I don't recommend that anyone with less than 200 talks or presentations behind him attempts it. A moment comes when there is nothing more to be said, and then the speaker needs to be able to 'hold the silence' in the room, instead of filling the air with more words. What is called for then is simply stillness and quietness while what has just been spoken hangs in the air, resonating in the audience's ears like the deep note of a bell. It takes confidence and authority to stand on a stage and hold a silence like that—perhaps to invite people *into* that silence—for as much as five seconds. It takes confidence and authority and experience to be able to manage the emotion in the room through pace, rhythm, volume, vocabulary and timing.

A powerful leader is skilled in creating dramatic moments that capture people's attention. He constructs such events as a theatre director might, manipulating the audience so that they notice the climax and are affected by it. He pays attention to his props and stage settings and (as I observed above) every aspect of his front stage, not merely the script. In mastering these things he acquires considerable power, of course, which can be misused; and it behoves him to use it with self-awareness, responsibility and restraint.

Using weak force. Learning to use weak force is no less of a challenge, but once again we can work to develop the necessary skills.

Emotional space: Using weak power—for example, in order to practise Consensual or Serving leadership—involves having sufficient emotional space ourselves to 'contain' other people's emotions. We choose to open our own emotional selves, like a garden without walls, so we can welcome in other people and the feelings or issues they may have, rather than keeping them outside, detached and managed. A good example is when a child has a tantrum and his father resists his own feelings and becomes a container to hold the child's feelings. Some key prerequisites for this are:

- Keeping the posture of your body open, rather than closed or aggressive
- Reflecting the other person's emotions back to them ('I can see you're feeling very angry about this...'). Tone as well as content is important in doing this—so that you echo that anger (say) in your voice rather than merely commenting on it in a detached and neutral way.
- Inviting the other person to say a little more about the situation ('Could you say a bit more about that?')
- Exploring their feelings ('And how does it make you feel when I do that?')
- Asking them to help you change the situation ('What do you feel I could do now to make things better?')

Emotional containment: The psychotherapist Margo Sunderland explains what goes on chemically in the brain when a person is 'emotionally contained' in this way. Asking an angry man (say) to express his feelings provides a release for the pressure that built up while he felt no one was listening to him. When he feels a resonance with another person and believes he has been heard and accepted by them, his need to be defensive or aggressive diminishes and the adrenaline that flooded his body during his outburst begins rapidly to subside. Offering to help him stimulates the flow of positive-attachment chemicals such as serotonin and creates a virtuous cycle of positive emotions rather than a 'stress cycle'.

Finally, Sunderland suggests, physically touching him will reconnect him to others and make a dangerous situation safe again. One of the things that will have triggered the release of adrenaline is that during his outburst he knew he had crossed a boundary and was out of control and that felt dangerous. The adrenaline flows and aggravates both his defensiveness and his aggression. Making him feel safe again is important to break this cycle.[9]

2. Learn when to use each strategy

There is obviously no point in being able to use different strategies but not knowing *when* to use them. This is a matter of reading a situation accurately. A former aide to Henry Kissinger recalls that three questions would be asked when Richard Nixon's administration addressed any issue at its daily conferences. They were these:

- · What is actually happening right now?
- · What is likely to happen next?
- · What will A do if B does X?

Those three simple questions highlight what good strategy is all about: knowing what is actually going on (rather that guessing, or being content to be ignorant), being able to predict where things are likely to go and being able to forecast what kind of reaction any action will provoke. This is basic systems thinking. It works because it is not too complicated. Of course, what it requires is both experience and a predictive model—experience of what has happened in the past and a model that enables you to predict the effect of doing X. This is the value of the concept of the ecology of power: it gives us a model that explains the fundamental structure of power in any social system. This enables us to identify, almost in a clinical way, all the different forces that could be brought to bear and it puts us in a strong position to predict how the system will react if B applies force Y to A.

Sadly, in our specialized age it is increasingly rare to find in any one single individual the mobility demonstrated by Archie McIndoe. One reason for this is that today we are encouraged by our educational curriculum and culture to divorce the social and the emotional from the intellectual. While we are still young, we are taught to think of these realms as entirely separate. Mathematics and the sciences on the one hand are 'hard', intellectual studies; the arts on the

---

[9] Margot Sunderland has created, with the aid of the artist Nicky Armstrong, the most engaging, delightful yet powerful set of resources for adults working with children who have emotional difficulties. Using stories and pictures, her books explore metaphors that enable children to express the feelings they have been repressing, and help adults to manage these feelings (as well as their own). See, for example, *Helping Children who Bottle Up Their Feelings/A Nifflenoo Called Nevermind* and *Helping Children who Have Hardened their Hearts or Become Bullies/A Wibble Called Bipley (and a Few Honks)* (Speechmark, 1999 and 2001 respectively)

other hand are 'soft' and expressive and engage the emotions. Doctors are not enabled to develop 'people skills', while nursing is regarded as a profession for the non-academic. Caring is removed from strategy, humour from execution, fellowship from delivery. By impressing this division on the young we polarize knowledge and may prevent children from developing the ability to 'know and lead' in a richer, more holistic way.

Leadership is one of the very few disciplines in which the *dis*integrated need to become reintegrated. The leader operates *not* within any one discipline but across the whole range of human encounter and meaning. The leader and her followers perform a kind of dance. At times, this is structured and disciplined and set moves are rehearsed, refined and co-ordinated. At other times, the dance is fluid and the dancers invent their own steps. Sometimes the dance breaks new ground, at other times its moves are familiar. At times it is fast, at other times stately, or even sombre. The dance can be both intimate and clinical, precise and fluid. The leader is not the leader of the dance but a partner in it—because it is something beyond us, in which (as T S Eliot put it) we 'must move in measure'.[10] Paradoxically, it is an experience in which time becomes timeless and movement becomes stillness.

Eight tips on how to develop greater mobility as a leader

1. Learn by experience. Take a leadership role—you will learn most about leadership by practising it.
2. Practise using different strategies. If there are some you know you have not developed, consciously create opportunitites to try them out.
3. Reflect on what happens when you use different strategies. The more you notice, the more you'll be able to change and develop.
4. Assemble a council of wise friends around you—a small, trusted group of people who know you well, are on your side and can help you to identify your blind spots. Give them permission to point out your areas of strength and weakness.
5. Serve. Every leader needs, as good practice, to have an area of her life in which she is not leading but being led. This might involve serving on a voluntary body (but not as leader!), taking on some menial tasks or helping out some people in need who have nothing to offer you in return.
6. Practise being still and 'attending to the moment' at different times in the day, rather than always looking ahead to the next step. You will notice more about what is actually going on.

---

[10] T S Eliot, 'Little Gidding', *Collected Poems 1909–1962* (Faber and Faber, this edition 1963)

7. Lay down your power at major junctions of your life. It's tempting to move from one high-powered role straight into another. Consider taking a sabbatical, when you will be out of the system and no one will call you. Only in this way will you discover whether you are truly free of the *need* to be powerful.

8. Be patient. You will probably find that, as you become more undefended, so your influence will grow. However, now may not be the time when you can use it most significantly. Often we need to wait quietly, learning to be content with what we have, before we are given the opportunity to make our greatest contribution (think of Churchill, Mandela and Reagan, among many others).

FIFTEEN

Leading with Nothing to Lose: the Key to Mobility

You might think, from the previous chapter, that the freedom to be mobile is simply a matter of acquiring the skills and experience to do so. You might be forgiven for concluding that this is just another book offering yet more tips on how to be the most competent and effective leader possible. You might also feel confused. The title of this book is *The Undefended Leader: Leading with Nothing to Lose*, but am I not simply providing another set of arms so that leaders can be better defended, not less?

If the skills I have talked about were to make us more potent and less vulnerable as leaders, then yes, that would be true. However, if those skills are not for *our* benefit, not to defend *us*, but instead are acquired for the benefit of the people we serve, the answer is 'No'. Then they are not assets we exploit but gifts we give to others. The difference here lies in the fundamental freedom of the leader as a person. Every single one of us has emotional needs. The message of the first book of this trilogy, *Leading out of Who You Are*, was that unless those needs are met in the context of a relationship with an Other who accepts us unconditionally, we will seek to meet them from human relationships around us. When a leader does this, she starts to exploit her followers as a surrogate source of affection, power, control, belonging or whatever it may be she needs. Her followers cease to be people she is freely serving and instead, to some extent, become commodities she needs and uses. The transaction between leader and followers becomes corrupted and, rather than freedom, it results in a kind of collusion.

The undefended leader is the one whose needs are met through an unconditional attachment to an Other, in which she finds identity, belonging and affection. This source of approval gives her such security that her sense of self is not defined by her success as a leader. Who she is is not determined by the response of the audience she is performing in front of. As a result, she is free to play the role of leader without having any personal interest in earning applause. Instead, she can act generously, both in attending to the needs of her audience and in serving them freely, with courage and commitment.

Anyone who is attached to success and results, for example, may be unable to practise the reserved, weak strategies of leadership, Self-emptying (RWC) and Serving (RWX), which require an attitude of service and a readiness to relinquish control. I remember working with the leader of a large church. He had been in post for about a year and had followed a pastor who had nurtured the congregation so well over the years that it had grown considerably. However, now that growth had stopped and many of the church's activities were slightly tired and dry. People desperately needed a fresh start and a renewed vision. However, this would have involved discontinuing some of the activities. 'I can't just stop them,' the new pastor said to me one day as we were discussing the options. 'If I did that, what would people think? That I wasn't as good a leader as my predecessor?' His fear of damaging his image, of being seen as less effective, prevented this man from adopting the Self-emptying and Serving strategies the church so desperately needed. The result was that it did not begin to grow again.

Likewise, anyone who is frightened of failing may be unable to practise the presented, strong strategies of leadership, Commanding (PSC) and Pacesetting (PSX), which require a willingness to run the risk of missing the targets they set. I recall another leader who consistently failed to impose the controls on the front stage of his organization that were necessary for it to be as productive as it could have been. The reason for this was that he felt more comfortable using the Visionary strategy, inspiring a vibrant, imaginative community, and was unwilling to take control of the front stage. He feared that if he did, the organization would lose some of its authenticity and creativity. The result was frequent conflict with his board. They wasted energy and money, and he didn't receive the trust and support he wanted.

Ultimately, it is not a matter of competence that enables a leader to become mobile but a matter of inner security and personal freedom. I remember a conversation I had with the head of a large school in London as we discussed a problem of leadership one day over a drink after work. 'But, Simon,' he said, 'how possible really is it to change? I mean, you maintain that each of us can learn to use other strategies, but, given that we have all been using the same old, familiar strategies for years, and given that they have worked OK for us and we feel safe with them, is it really possible to change them, now at my age? It's a great idea, but is it realistic?'

This is a crucial question. If it is not possible actually to change, why should we bother at all? The answer is this: I think it is possible to change, but it's not just a matter of being willing to learn or developing new skills. Certainly, these are both important factors, but they are not the most important. In fact, the most important thing is stillness. 'You see, Ben,' I told him, 'the only way I will possibly let go of my strategies, which I know so well, which I'm so comfortable with, which give me a sense of safety and also—let's be honest—power and control, is if I reach that point of stillness where what I needed to achieve by using them no longer matters to me like it did. It's a matter of letting them go. You see, most of my day I am busy focused on my task, trying to get my jobs done, running frantically from one thing to the next. I don't notice what's really going on around me—I've got a hundred things in my head, I haven't got time to stop and reflect about how I feel, let alone how others feel. Of course, I carry on doing the same thing, day after day. The only way I will change is if I am able first to stop. Before change comes stillness.

'Imagine', I went on, 'what would happen if you were still for a moment—truly still. Not just inactive, but still in your heart. You let go of your ambition, your desires and personal hopes, and instead paid attention to the situation in front of you. You allowed yourself to become open to what was going on around: the moods, the fears, the energy of all that was happening around you, in the office, at home, wherever you were. You paid attention to it. And now imagine that, instead of reacting in fear, you acted in freedom—freedom then to intervene in that situation and do whatever was needed.'

'But', Ben replied, 'how could you ever achieve that stillness in the first place?'

'You can only find that stillness if your own needs have first been met. If I'm still worried about my own success or reputation, then I'm dominated by fear—fear of what I might lose or suffer. I need to have that fear quelled, and that anxiety assuaged. And that can happen only if I'm confident of being loved: secure in a relationship in which I know who I am, and which can't be jeopardized by anything I may do or not do. Then I am safe enough to be still.'

The upshot of all this is that the freedom to move anywhere, to use all of the leadership strategies, is available only to those who can freely face personal loss without fear. Or, to use the language of the ecology of power, only those people who have themselves experienced self-emptying, who have reached the point where they lay everything down and let go of power, and have accepted their vulnerability and sought security instead in another kind of relationship, only these are truly free to lead.

In terms of power, Christians have tended to regard the death of Jesus on the cross as a mystery. They recognize it as a sacrifice through which their sins are forgiven, and appreciate that it is at the heart of the Christian message. They know, too, that it is the mainspring of their own response to God of gratitude and faith. However, they can't make out how it might impinge on their understanding of power. As a result, they continue to exploit power in much the same way as they did before they become followers of Jesus. They believe that churches should be well organized and managed. They advocate the use of the best resources to promote church growth and send their pastors on training courses to become more effective evangelists, teachers and executives. They read books on executive leadership and want the church to learn from the business world how to be more successful, how to grow faster. They pore over strategies that promise greater church growth much as a CEO might pore over books that promise an increase in corporate profits if he just follows this system or that.

Jesus used many leadership strategies in the course of his ministry: he could be Commanding when confronting his opponents, Consensual when nurturing his group of followers, Foundational when expounding the Law and establishing the basics of his message. In fact, he could and did use all of the eight strategies—if you wanted, you could easily make an analysis of how he used each one in different circumstances and for different purposes. However, in the moment when he achieved his greatest triumph, in the act that changed the world, he brought to bear not competence or strength or force, but weakness. He emptied himself of power and died on a cross.

Some Christians would like to see God as the Great Executive in the sky. Many church leaders regard themselves as eager junior managers, running his operation for him; as a devoted salesforce, racking up the converts; as a committed customer-care department, providing superlative pastoral oversight; as a forward-thinking training-and-development division, improving staff performance. What they fail to grasp is that God chooses not to work through executive strategies without first going through the suffering of death and resurrection. The death of Jesus on the cross was not a one-off, an out-of-character gesture by God, like a heavenly curve ball. No, it was the very paradigm of how he acts. Giving up his life in an act of self-emptying, so that it could be given back again, more powerful than before—this exemplifies the way that God continually chooses to act. Yes, he can use other strategies of power. Yes, he knows all they can achieve. Yes, he understands that a healthy human society needs foundations and commands, social capital, vision and drive. However, he also knows that unless people are willing to participate in death and resurrection, they will remain trapped in a system that is based not on freedom but on fear. The process of self-emptying is not merely one of the eight different leadership strategies: it is the foundation of all the others, the key that unlocks them all, the sacrifice that consecrates them all.

A willingness to embrace weakness is utterly characteristic of the God that is portrayed in the Bible. In contrast to how other world religions conceive him, the distinctive Christian understanding of God is that his priority is for the underdog: the poor, the meek, the broken, the outcast. It seems that the depth of his love is revealed most fully not in power but in the brokenness of Jesus, on a cross. And it is for that reason (and that alone) that any leader seeking to 'lead as Jesus led', seeking to implement a vision of leadership informed by faith— whether in the church or in business, in the family or in government—must be equally willing to embrace weakness.

Again, I need to make it clear I am not talking about weakness as an end in itself. Self-emptying, laying down power, is merely a channel through which a great power is allowed to flow—but it is power that enables others to flourish, not power to aggrandize us. Peggy Noonan observed how crucial Reagan's own experiences of weakness and failure were in forming him as a man and as a leader. 'I like to remember this: Reagan played Vegas. In 1954, when demand for his acting services was slowing, Reagan emceed a variety act to make money and keep his name in the air. He didn't like doing it. But it was what he had to do, so he did it. The point is he knew what it was to be through, to have people not answer your calls. When I thought about this time in his life once, I thought, All the great ones have known failure, but only the greatest of the great use it. He always used his. It deepened him and sharpened him. ... He didn't become President to reach some egocentric sense of personal destiny; he didn't need the presidency, and he didn't go for it because of some strange vanity, some weird desire to be loved or a need of power to fill the empty spaces within. He didn't want the presidency in order to be a big man. He wanted the presidency so that he could do big things.'

Freedom is the jewel that is shaped by such self-emptying, and it has three beautifully-honed facets. The first facet is *freedom from the need to be great.* Almost all leaders have a desire to be great—to dominate their world and leave their mark on history. Such atavistic drives spur us on and summon from us the sacrifices that are often required to achieve such goals. However, the greatest glory remains for those who have conquered such ambition. Only when you are content to be used or not used, wanted or not wanted, can you truly serve others without at the same time exploiting them. Only then can you truly enable others to flourish and become great without regarding them as a threat.

The second facet is *the freedom to be fully available*. One of the greatest gifts a leader can give to others is the space within herself to contain their feelings. This is a matter of listening, of taking into ourselves the needs of others, absorbing them and sharing in them without being overwhelmed by them. This kind of listening is the basis of true friendship, if not of all human relationships. We pay therapists billions of dollars a year to do just this—and yet at heart the role they play is only what is properly human. Listening to someone else without jumping in with our own answers, being still enough to hear without being distracted, being patient enough to give them time to untangle their confusion, being open enough to accept them wherever they are, being wise enough to see their situation in the context of a wider narrative—these are the greatest gifts one person can give to another. They lie at the heart of what it means truly to lead another person.

If we ourselves have unmet emotional needs, we are, paradoxically, 'full up' with our own emotions—and in that event we won't have room for anyone else's. I know all too well that when I come home from leading a course all day I am pretty full emotionally: I have spent the day 'containing' the emotions of many other people and haven't paid attention to my own. If my children start fighting and hurting each other, I have very little space to contain their feelings and often just want to put the lid straight back on them. If we are to listen to others in the way I have been describing, we ourselves need a container in which to place our own feelings. This relationship may be a human one, but it is my contention that a relationship with a divine Father who himself is 'emotionally big enough' is the only thing that can securely contain all our feelings.

The third, and perhaps most wonderful, facet of the jewel of freedom is *the freedom to lead with nothing to lose*. Think back to the time when you did best something that you love doing—perhaps singing in a choir, or acting on a stage, or giving a piano recital, or sailing a boat, or playing in a sports team. I would bet that your finest performance was when you were most free of the fear of failure. This is certainly true for me. When I was free to concentrate totally, to be completely absorbed in what I was doing, to give myself to it, with abandon, with no anxiety about the outcome, those were the times when I have given my most noteworthy performances. When we lead with something to lose, whether it be our reputation, our position, our salary or whatever, we lead with our guards up. Of course, this may mean we are totally focused—I would not deny that—but always some of our energy is being consumed by the self-protective self-monitoring that goes on when we are trying to evaluate our performance even as we give it. Leading with nothing to lose liberates us from fear and gives us an abandoned freedom to give everything we have to what we are doing.

Paradoxically, when we reach this position we achieve a kind of stillness in which we are free to pay attention to what is really going on around us. Stillness in the eye of a storm results in a deeper awareness, an ability to listen to the moment—and this in turn enables us to join in with what is truly important, right and good. And when we do this, we have the necessary mobility to lead appropriately—whether to act with strength or weakness, on the front stage or the back, to expand or consolidate. In this way, our freedom does indeed become manifest in our supremely enhanced performance, as we are able to choose to do whatever needs to be done, in whatever way is called for.

SIXTEEN

The Hospitality of the Undefended Leader

YOU AS HOST

DRAW YOUR OWN PICTURE

Mark and I were discussing current ideas about leadership. Like me, Mark worked with leaders, helping them to become more aware of their effect on others around them.

'On the one hand,' he said, 'there's the idea of the leader as hero, strong, capable, brave, who takes problems on and overcomes them. And then, on the other, there's Greenleaf's idea of "servant leadership". They seem to be at two ends of a scale. One is about power, the other about passivity. One is about dominating, the other seems to be about letting others dominate. Neither quite seems to capture what leadership is all about.'

I agreed. 'Neither concept is quite full enough or rich enough, is it?' I suggested. 'Leading others involves more than either of those two polarities. Of course, there are times when you do both of those things, but you do a lot more, too.' We had met up to talk about a possible new way of thinking about what a leader really needs to be, which we believed might be a better model than either hero or servant. We were exploring the idea that, at its heart, leadership is really most a matter of being a host.

You see, one of the problems with the model of hero or servant is that it focuses attention on the nature of the leader and her fundamental assets. Yet leading other people is actually about the space between the leader and her followers. It's about the relationships she creates and manages. If you think of a leader not as a hero or a servant but as a host, you immediately think in terms not of her fundamental assets but of the space she creates around her. You can't think about a host without thinking about a party, or a home, to which guests are welcomed. You start to think about the relationships that already exist, the friendships that may be formed. You start to think about leadership in terms of encounter and conversation.

This book has explored eight different leadership strategies, each of which 'does something' to the space around you. Used in concert, they offer a repertoire of social and emotional skills that allow a host to create and sustain a healthy, enriching, dynamic and (most importantly) humane space in which people can grow and give of their best. There are several basic ingredients in this task of hosting:

- Creating a safe space in which people can relax, confident that they understand what is going on and what is expected of them
- Facilitating encounters between people in which genuine listening can occur, and encouraging conversation, laughter and the exchange of ideas and possibilities, so that people leave enriched
- Giving the occasion meaning, structure and a sense of significance through sharing in rituals and traditions (playing games, saying grace, drinking toasts, asking people to sign a visitors' book...)

Each of these elements is important if the guests are to enjoy the experience and be enriched by it. They all fit into the eight strategies of leadership, which underlines how close the parallels are between the role of host and the role of leader. Each of the eight strategies provides ways in which the 'leadership host' can create the right social and emotional space around himself. Ideally, they are used in concert by a leader who is fully attentive to their effect, and the character of the space they are helping to create. He takes responsibility for shaping the overall character of this space and brings out the best in other people by making them feel welcome and at home.

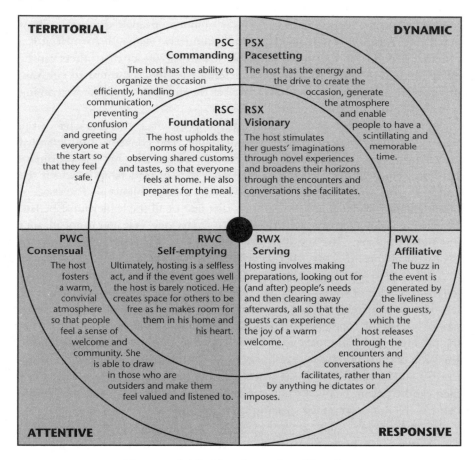

Diagram 16.1: The dynamics of hosting

Arguably, a leader can rarely offer genuine 'hospitality' if she insists on retaining control over everything that is going on. How miserable it is as a guest to feel that you can't walk where you like in the garden, you have to do exactly what your host has planned for you and you're going to be watched the whole time. A hospitable leader 'creates space' for others to express themselves and their gifts in shaping the 'landscape' of the occasion. She trusts them, and enjoys seeing them involved in this way—it's a source of delight to her that this is a collaborative endeavour. The greatest leadership always establishes freedom rather than control and is not too worried about results. It measures success not in terms of output or productivity but of the freedom others have to contribute—the way guests are drawn out of themselves and into the community.

Undefended leadership is about that kind of generous hospitality: a giving of ourselves to the world that transforms it, an opening-up of space in our lives in which the 'other' is welcomed and, indeed, utterly changed. As such, it is a task that depends on the 'space' available within the leader that others can be invited into. The quest to become undefended leaders is a quest to cultivate this interior space within ourselves, as well as the fluency to become welcoming hosts who can enrich our guests.

We've come to accept an idea of leadership in which the character of the leader is virtually irrelevant to his task as leader. The concept of undefended leadership contradicts this and insists that the right character is the primary attribute required. We've come to accept an idea of leadership in which the leader is strong and powerful and 'does things' for her followers. The concept of undefended leadership, however, says that first of all the leader must be led. Leadership is not a primary activity but a secondary one. A leader is not a leader first but a follower. First and foremost, she must be focused on the source of the love and grace that gives her security and sets her free.

Undefended leadership subverts expectations of power and self-sufficiency in favour of a life of vulnerability and dependence. It declares that the first steps taken by the undefended leader may not be on the metalled road to the training school but on the rough path of personal discipleship. It is on that journey that the process of formation is begun. Undefended leadership begins not with the amassing of skills and the acquisition of power but with the humility of learning to trust and to receive. It insists that the leader must begin by receiving. Only then can he go on, enabled to give to others. It is only out of this kind of life that the freedom and power to act greatly can come.

The language of hospitality draws our attention beyond issues of personal leadership towards wider horizons. How hospitable is the society we live in? To what extent does it create safe space in which very different people can not only enjoy a resilient coexistence but can also trust each other? How far does it protect the vulnerable? How far does it enrich the human spirit by promoting the highest virtues? To what extent is it founded on principles of generosity, trust and collective and personal responsibility? To what degree are those same qualities exhibited in its citizens?

Our exploration of the nature of power in undefended leadership has brought us to the frontiers of social and political leadership. Now we must ask the question: What would an undefended *society* look like? This is the territory I cover in the final book of this trilogy: What if the same parameters of hospitality were applied to a state? With such an ideal in mind, perhaps we could ask ourselves what sort of political, economic and even military choices we might make. Perhaps we could approach the major, pressing issues of our day with the same questions to help us: How could a principle of hospitality inform our country's policy on immigration? Or climate change? Or intervention overseas? Or education? Or the arts and media? Or business and private enterprise? Or religion and faith? Or medical ethics? Or civic responsibility?

If it's good to live in a home or work in a company that shows hospitality, perhaps it may also be good to live in a society that is founded on the same principles. Of course, such a proposition needs to be thought through very carefully. Families, and even companies, are relatively simple communities, but a society is far more complex and variegated. We would need to consider, for example, what it might mean for wealth creation and ownership. We'd need to look at the political mechanisms that distribute power, at the role of the constitution, written or unwritten, and the foundations of the state. We'd need to think about the nature of education, the principles underlying the formation of socially responsible adults. We'd need to reflect on the issues of rights and responsibilities, freedom and duty, and on how our society gives permission and approval. We'd need to examine all of these, and many other, facets of our society in order to try to understand how it functioned as a whole, as a social *system*.

However, we should be confident that principles that have proved true and good and strong at both a personal and an organizational level will also prove true, good and strong at a societal level. It has been worth taking pains to understand the nature of power in the simple transactions between an individual leader and his followers, because we may be able to apply our knowledge also to more complex situations. For example, we could analyse not just individual behaviour but that of a whole society in terms of the front stage and the back stage. We could differentiate the use of strong and weak power not just by individuals but by whole demographic groups, and could assess whether different sectors of the population were driven to expand or to consolidate. Indeed, it might be possible to build up a dynamic and yet coherent picture of our whole social system in these basic terms.

And if this were possible, the rewards might be great. Many of the big, unresolved and urgent questions of our day require just such a systemic analysis. We need to look at the whole, rather than just individual parts. We need to understand, for example, the impact our country's trade policy has right across society—on the 'underclass' as well as on the business elite. Likewise, we need to understand how its education policy affects the nation's economic future as well as our own children's welfare, and how its security policy impinges on our social cohesion as well as on our personal safety. Each individual thread is part of a much bigger picture, and if we try to pull it out we risk spoiling the whole tapestry.

As we come to the end of this second part of the trilogy, we turn our attention from questions of personal and organizational leadership to questions of social and political leadership—questions whose answers are going to determine the context for all our lives for years, if not decades, to come.

Appendix: Troubleshooting Problems in Leadership and Other FAQs

Now that we understand a little more about the mechanics of power in any social system, we may be able to apply these insights to different circumstances to achieve the results we need. Some of the most frequently asked questions about building organizations, teams and communities we can address effectively simply by following the principles suggested by the ecology of power and using the right strategies at the right time.

Here are some of the FAQs I have encountered, both in leading my own organizations and when advising others.

Q. *I'm trying to build a new business, and it seems to me important to establish the right culture at the outset. How do I do that?*

A. Your new business needs foundations. You've probably got a business plan to lay out the financial and commercial foundations, but what you also need is a 'culture plan' to lay out the social and emotional foundations. This is NOT the same as an organizational map that shows who is managed by who. It's a plan you draw up to establish the culture of the organization over the coming months. It must address the following questions:

- What are your foundations going to be? You need to establish core values, expected behaviours, standards, goals, routines and rhythms. Are you clear about yours?
- How are you planning to build these foundations so that they're all agreed and owned? You need to begin by creating opportunities to speak to all your teams face-to-face. Put a presentation together. Get their feedback. Make yourself available for comments. Check that everyone buys into them—get them to sign up! Train your managers to implement these foundational principles and practices with absolute consistency.
- How are you going to reinforce these foundations over time? Invent ways to remind everyone of these principles and practices every year. Think about how you integrate new staff so they are familiar with them—use a buddy system to teach them.

Don't over-manage your staff! If they're not doing what they should, don't do it for them—and don't axe them. Instead, get them to look again at the charter they signed up to, identify where things have gone wrong and put it right.

A final point: you will probably find you have to reinterpret your basic principles for every new phase of your business's growth. Be flexible—but remember the foundations you said the business was built on in the first place. Then you will have a business you can be proud of.

Q. *I'm in a real battle for survival. The market has turned down, sales have fallen and my staff are getting anxious about their futures. What should I do?*

A. There may be ways in which you need to look at the market and see where it's going in the future. If you can't adjust the service you provide to fit the new demand, you may be in trouble.

However, in the short term you need to hold your nerve *and* help your staff to hold theirs. This is a matter of Commanding leadership. Imagine that you're Ernest Shackleton leading an Antarctic expedition: the weather has turned against you, your rations are low and people's lives are in danger. You need to plot a course for survival. What do you do?

- You give people confidence that you can make decisions and can protect them. Now is the time to stand tall, look people in the eye and tell them the truth.
- Explain the sacrifices you're all going to have to make to survive (job cuts, reductions in expense accounts, other cutbacks, consolidation). Explain why they need to make these sacrifices and the benefits of doing so.
- Explain very clearly the next immediate task—that is, what you all need to achieve today in order to survive till tomorrow. And the same tomorrow. And the same the next day.
- Explain the route you're plotting out of the mess, step by step, so they know exactly what is happening and when.
- Keep close to your troops—remember that Commanding PSC leadership needs to be supported by a Serving RWX style. Spend more time face-to-face with them, be present in the office and be seen to be making sacrifices yourself. Make people coffee. Find things to celebrate. Little things like that keep people's spirits up.
- Build camaraderie by encouraging people to share ideas, resources and so forth. Consider buddying people together so no one feels alone. In these situations, you will either develop tremendous camaraderie or run the risk of mutiny or desertion. Use your instinctive team-builders to create the former and prevent the latter!

Q. *We have a team that needs to perform really effectively over the next 12 months. If they can rise to the challenge, we have a real opportunity to break into a new level of business. What should I be doing to ensure they achieve that level of performance?*

A. Developing teams that perform exceptionally well is all about creating a virtuous circle of energy, drive, discipline and self-belief. The key is to get the circle started. Here's how to do it:

- Teams work best when they are fired up by a vision that motivates them. You need to use RSX leadership to find the critical thing that will excite your team—it may be the pride of achieving something unprecedented, it may be financial success, it may be new opportunities that flow from success, it may be a higher purpose they would be fulfilling. Find the vision, focus it and project it—and refer to it consistently as the mountaintop to which you're all heading.

- The vision will create a sense of community. Use a PWC strategy to capitalize on this. Create a sense of privilege, intimacy and camaraderie in the team. Mark them out as different, so they know it. Foster a culture of mutual encouragement and community by getting them to talk to each other every week, sharing ideas and thoughts.

- Give them team incentives, in Affiliative style. That is, instead of individual incentives, reward the whole team when one of them does well. This motivates them all to help each other to succeed.

- Their energy, drive and discipline will inspire the hope that the vision can be realized, and thus a virtuous circle is created, for as the vision gets stronger, so does the sense of community and so does the energizing sense of self-belief.

One warning! Once you have created a team like this, you'll find it hard to separate them and they may become a maverick unit in your organization. You need to think about how you are going to integrate them with other teams in the future to avoid them becoming potentially rebellious.

Q. *For years, we've been asking for more independence from our parent organization. They are so controlling and refuse to recognize our desire to take responsibility and have greater autonomy. The effect is demoralizing. What should we do?*

A. If things are as bad as that, it sounds as if you're reaching the point where a more radical approach is called for. First, though, you need to make sure there really is no way your parent organization could cut you some slack. Have you found out why they won't do this? Have you demonstrated that you could manage on your own?

Once you have clarified this, you need to gauge just how strongly your staff want the change. How desperate are they? What are they prepared to do? And to give up, perhaps? In other words, how much would they really hate it if things remained as they are? Many people talk about change but in reality lack the fight to make it happen. This is about using an RWX approach that listens to your staff on the ground.

If you are clear that there is sufficient support, you have two options. Both of these employ RWC force, and both are inflammatory and entail risk.

First, you could simply cease to comply with your parent organization. This is the equivalent of passive resistance or civil disobedience. You're not downing tools, you're not going on strike, you're simply refusing to recognize their authority over you. You get on with your work, deliver results, but you do it outside their jurisdiction. Expect things to get hot! It will provoke a reaction and you'll find you're forcing your parent organization either to clamp down or to start negotiating. Either way, they will realize you mean business. You keep the moral high ground by continuing to work, and you hope that ultimately this will make them see sense.

Your other option is to withdraw. If you really feel you can make a better job of it alone, go and do it! Take the staff who want to go with you and start up a rival company. As long as you abide by the restrictions in your contracts, there's nothing to stop you doing this. Maybe it's time to put your money where your mouth is.

Q. *I'd like help with general troubleshooting. Often, I'm faced with teams that seem a bit stuck: they're demotivated, apathetic, just kind of run out of gas. Mostly they become cynical, and then bitchy at the same time. As a result, they're not only unproductive but also a negative influence on others in the organization. What should I do about such teams?*

A. Most problems with teams lie with their foundations. If you build a house and give it only one-foot-deep foundations, pretty soon you'll start to notice cracks in the walls as it begins to subside. The problem is not in the walls, or in the architecture necessarily: it's in the structural engineering—what has not been done underground. Teams become apathetic when they have no clear sense of where they're going, why they're doing what they're doing and whether it can be achieved. They may be worn out, they may not think their work is worthwhile, they may not think it is doable. All you can do is embark on the messy and time-consuming work of digging up the foundations of the structure and underpinning it.

· You need to examine your expectations of the team. Do you have strong foundations?

- If so, to what extent do the team know about them and consent to them? If you have never communicated those values, expectations, boundaries and so on, they won't know about them. If you simply imposed them at the outset as 'This is what I want to happen,' they may never have given them their consent.

- Get the team together and broach the subject of the problem. Admit that something is wrong and see if they acknowledge it, too. Tell them what the problem is on your side—that is, how it is affecting you, the organization, productivity and so on—and let them tell you what the problem is on their side.

- As you start to understand the problem, get them to reflect on the foundations—the shared expectations—that underlie your enterprise and their team. Do they still agree with them? Do they matter to them any more?

- You may find that at this stage some people say these foundations no longer matter to them in the same way. Fair enough, people change— but in this team you ONLY have people to whom the agreed objectives really matter. Thus, you make it clear to the dissidents you need to work with them to find them a role they do believe in, because they can't remain in this team. This is a team in which everyone agrees to aim towards the specified goals in the ways agreed. Otherwise, they're letting everyone else down.

- Then, having strengthened the foundations of purpose and expectations, removed any cause for further subsidence and dealt with the rubble, you have to establish whether there is anything YOU need to do differently to support them better. 'What do *I* need to change to ensure you can get your work done?' It may be to provide more direct support, or more training, resources or time...

- Finally, you all agree the new basis on which you're going to work. You make a commitment to it, and agree to review it in a month, then in three months, then a year.

If things don't improve, it may be time to think about winding the team down. Every group has a natural lifespan, and this one may just have reached the end of theirs.

Select Bibliography

Peter G Bourne. *Jimmy Carter: A Comprehensive Biography From Plains to Post-Presidency.* New York, Scribner, 1997

Clayton Carson, ed. *The Autobiography of Martin Luther King.* Abacus, 1999

Richard J Carwardine. *Lincoln.* Pearson Educational/Longman, 2003

Roy Jenkins. *Churchill: A Biography.* Farrar, Straus and Giroux, 2001

Nelson Mandela. *Long Walk to Freedom: The Autobiography of Nelson Mandela.* Little Brown & Co, 1994

Henri J M Nouwen. *The Wounded Healer: Ministry in Contemporary Society.* Doubleday, 1972

Richard Reeves. *President Reagan: The Triumph of Imagination.* New York, Simon & Schuster, 2005

Anthony Sampson. *Mandela: The Authorized Biography.* Random House, 2000

Robert A Strong. *Working in the World: Jimmy Carter and the Making of American Foreign Policy.* Baton Rouge, Louisiana State University, 2000

— "Recapturing leadership: The Carter Administration and the Crisis of Confidence", *Presidential Studies Quarterly* 16, Fall 1986

Philip Yancey. *The Jesus I Never Knew.* Zondervan, 2002

The Leadership Community and Leadership Signature Profile™

The Leadership Community

Simon Walker's The Undefended Leader trilogy developed out of his work with a number of leaders in business, charity, politics or the church who make up an on-line community, The Leadership Community. The Community is an ongoing association which is supported by a website (www.theleadershipcommunity. org). It provides many resources for those who want to offer undefended leadership, including training courses, conferences, web tools and on-line discussion forums. You can become a free guest member of the community through a simple online registration process.

The Leadership Community is committed to practice: we are members because we are trying to *live out* a certain kind of life. The only condition of membership is that you choose to join us.

The Leadership Signature Profile™*

If you are in leadership, you may benefit from profiling your *own leadership signature*. We have developed a unique, web-based psychometric tool, The Leadership Signature Profile™ which can do this quickly, accurately and with helpful feedback.

The Leadership Signature Profile™ has been authored by Simon Walker and uniquely analyses:
- which of the eight leadership strategies you use as your default,
- the range of strategies you use in competitive, conflict and crisis situations as a leader,
- your unique signature as a leader.

---

* The Leadership Signature Profile™ is a subsidiary product of The PEP Arena™ which was developed by Simon Walker at Oxford University in 2002. The PEP Arena is a proprietary tool of Human Ecology and has won several UK awards.

The Leadership Signature Profile™ will:

- present your results in a clear five-page report on how you lead in calm, competitive, conflict and crisis situations.
- align your leadership signature with the great world leaders in the book
- provide a insightful report on the behaviours, issues and development areas you may have in your leadership
- highlight ways to develop your signature to be more effective as a leader
- link you directly to the right exercises and resources from The Leadership Community that are tailored to support your development as a leader.

**Visit www.theleadershipcommunity.org
for more information about the benefits and costs of
The Leadership Signature Profile™, and to use it.**

Other titles in
The Undefended Leader trilogy
by Simon Walker

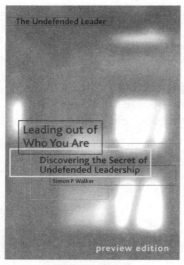

**LEADING OUT OF
WHO YOU ARE**

*Discovering the Secret of Undefended
Leadership*

ISBN: 978 1903689 43 1

**LEADING WITH
EVERYTHING TO GIVE**

*Disarming the Powers and
Authorities*

ISBN: 978 1 903689 455

*"Leadership is commonly associated with dominance and
power. Simon Walker shows that there are other types of
leadership capable of being more effective."*

R Meredith Belbin*

P̓QUANT
editions
www.piquanteditions.com

---

*R Meredith Belbin, a previous chairman of the Industrial Training Research Unit and founder
member of Belbin Associates, is the author of several management titles, including *The Coming
Shape of Organization* (1996).